STAR WARS™

GRAPHICS

EXPLORE *STAR WARS* AND *THE FORCE AWAKENS* THROUGH INFOGRAPHICS

EGMONT
We bring stories to life

Star Wars Graphics first published in Great Britain 2016
by Egmont UK Limited © & ™ 2016 Lucasfilm Ltd.

Star Wars The Force Awakens Graphics first published in Great Britain 2016
by Egmont UK Limited © & ™ 2016 Lucasfilm Ltd.

This edition published in Great Britain 2017
by Egmont UK Limited, The Yellow Building,
1 Nicholas Road, London W11 4AN
© & ™ 2017 Lucasfilm Ltd.

ISBN 978 0 6035 7407 8
67913/1
Printed in China

For more great *Star Wars* books, visit www.egmont.co.uk/starwars

Stay safe online. Any website addresses listed in this book are correct at the time of going to print. However, Egmont is
not responsible for content hosted by third parties. Please be aware that online content can be subject to change and websites
can contain content that is unsuitable for children. We advise that all children are supervised when using the internet.

STAR WARS™
GRAPHICS

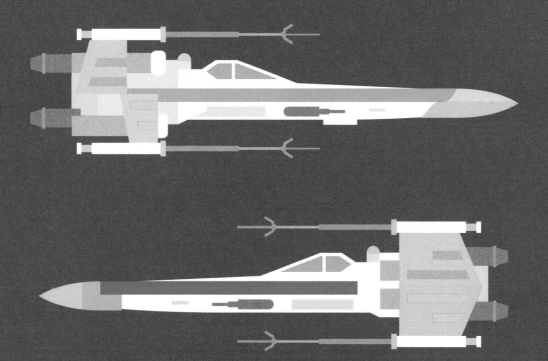

EXPLORE *STAR WARS* AND *THE FORCE AWAKENS*
THROUGH INFOGRAPHICS

CONTENTS

GENERAL INFORMATION

FIRST TRILOGY

EPISODE IV — A NEW HOPE

EPISODE V — THE EMPIRE STRIKES BACK

EPISODE VI — RETURN OF THE JEDI

SECOND TRILOGY

EPISODE I – THE PHANTOM MENACE

EPISODE II – ATTACK OF THE CLONES

EPISODE III – REVENGE OF THE SITH

THE FORCE AWAKENS

A long time ago in a galaxy far, far away....

STAR WARS

INTRODUCTION

When *A New Hope* stormed into cinemas in 1977, nobody could have imagined it would spawn a franchise that would captivate fans for an entire generation. The latest instalment, *The Force Awakens*, brought back some of our favourite characters, and introduced us to new heroes, loveable rogues and loyal droids.

Although each new *Star Wars* film brings new stories and characters to the table, there are many links between the seven episodes that form a richly layered universe. This book aims to connect the past and present through engaging infographics.

Enjoy the graphics, and get ready for *The Last Jedi* and even more spectacular films to come.

GENERALINFORMATION

[1977-2005]

BESPIN

Biosphere :
gas, clouds
Diameter :
118,000 km
Natives :
Neo-Bespinians
Population :
6 million
Films :
Episodes V & VI

KAMINO

Biosphere :
oceans
Diameter :
19,270 km
Natives :
Kaminoans
Population :
1 million
Film :
Episode II

UTAPAU

Biosphere :
desert
Diameter :
12,900 km
Natives :
Utapauns
Population :
95 million
Film :
Episode III

KASHYYYK

Biosphere :
forests, plains
Diameter :
12,765 km
Natives :
Wookiees
Population :
45 million
Film :
Episode III

ALDERAAN

Biosphere :
forests, lakes, mountains
Diameter :
12,500 km
Natives :
Killiks
Population :
2 billion
Films :
Episodes III & IV

CORUSCANT

Biosphere :
urban
Diameter :
12,240 km
Natives :
humans
Population :
1 trillion
Films :
Episodes I, II, III & VI

NABOO

Biosphere :
plains, lakes
Diameter :
12,120 km
Natives :
Gungans
Population :
4.5 billion
Films :
Episodes I, II, III & VI

GEONOSIS

Biosphere :
rock, deserts, mountains
Diameter :
11,370 km
Natives :
Geonosians
Population :
100 billion
Film :
Episode II

Biosphere :
deserts
Diameter :
10,465 km
Natives :
Tuskens
Population :
80,000
Films :
Episodes I, II, III, IV & VI

TATOOINE

Biosphere :
forests
Diameter :
10,200 km
Natives :
Colonised
Population :
0–1000
Film :
Episode IV

YAVIN 4

Biosphere :
ice
Diameter :
10,088 km
Natives :
Lurmens
Population :
19 million
Film :
Episode III

MYGEETO

Biosphere :
mushroom forests
Diameter :
9,100 km
Natives :
Felucians
Population :
8.5 million
Film :
Episode III

FELUCIA

Biosphere :
swamps
Diameter :
8,900 km
Natives :
Hepsalum Tash
Population :
1
Films :
Episodes V & VI

DAGOBAH

Biosphere :
ice
Diameter :
7,200 km
Natives :
Skels
Population :
unknown
Film :
Episode V

HOTH

Biosphere :
forests
Diameter :
4,900 km
Natives :
Ewoks
Population :
30 million
Film :
Episode VI

ENDOR

Biosphere :
lava, volcanoes
Diameter :
4,200 km
Natives :
Mustafarians
Population :
20,000
Film :
Episode III

MUSTAFAR

MASTERS AND STUDENTS

"BUT WHICH WAS DESTROYED, THE MASTER OR THE APPRENTICE?" MACE WINDU ASKED YODA AT THE END OF *THE PHANTOM MENACE*. HERE IS A DIAGRAM WHICH WILL HELP YOU UNDERSTAND WHO TAUGHT WHAT TO WHOM.

12
JEDI IN THE
COUNCIL

5
SITH

2
JEDI
TURNED SITH

BBY - Before the Battle of Yavin

ABY - After the Battle of Yavin

Birth: 147–120 BBY
Death: 32 BBY
Species: Muun
Planet: Mygeeto

DARTH PLAGUEIS

MASTER: Darth Tenebrous
APPRENTICE: Darth Sidious

FILM(S)

I II III IV V VI

Birth: 82 BBY
Death: 4 ABY
Species: human   1.78 m
Planet: Naboo   75 kg

DARTH SIDIOUS

MASTER: Darth Plagueis
APPRENTICES: Darth Maul,
Darth Tyranus, Darth Vader

FILM(S)

I II III IV V VI

Birth: 54 BBY
Death: 2 BBY
Species: Dathomirian   1.75 m
Planet: Dathomir   80 kg

DARTH MAUL

MASTER: Darth Sidious
APPRENTICE: Savage Opress

FILM(S)

I II III IV V VI

Birth: 102 BBY
Death: 19 BBY
Species: human   1.93 m
Planet: Serenno   80 kg

DARTH TYRANUS

MASTERS: Yoda, Darth Sidious
APPRENTICES: Qui-Gon Jinn,
Asajj Ventress (dark Jedi),
Savage Opress (dark Jedi)

FILM(S)

I II III IV V VI

Birth: 41 BBY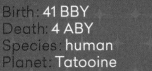
Death: 4 ABY
Species: human   2.02 m
Planet: Tatooine 136 kg

DARTH VADER

MASTER: Darth Sidious
APPRENTICE: ?

FILM(S)

I II III IV V VI

Birth: 41 BBY
Death: 4 ABY
Species: human   1.88 m
Planet: Tatooine 84 kg

ANAKIN SKYWALKER

MASTERS: Obi-Wan Kenobi,
Ki-Adi-Mundi
APPRENTICE: Ahsoka Tano

FILM(S)

I II III IV V VI

Birth: Unknown
Death: 19 BBY
Species: Dathomirian / Zabrak Iridonian
Planet: Nar Shaddaa
♂
1.71 m

EETH KOTH

MASTER: Kosul Ayada
APPRENTICE: Sharad Hett

FILM(S)

I   II   III   IV   V   VI

Birth: 72 BBY
Death: 19 BBY
Species: human
Planet: Haruun Kal
♂
1.88 m
84 kg

MACE WINDU

MASTERS: Yoda, T'ra Saa
APPRENTICES: Depa Billaba, Devan For'deschel, Echu Shen-Jon, Darrus Jeht

FILM(S)

I   II   III   IV   V   VI

Birth: Unknown
Death: 19 BBY
Species: human
Planet: Chalacta
♀
1.68 m

DEPA BILLABA

MASTER: Mace Windu

FILM(S)

I   II   III   IV   V   VI

Birth: 92 BBY
Death: 19 BBY
Species: Cerean
Planet: Cerea
♂
1.98 m
82 kg

KI-ADI-MUNDI

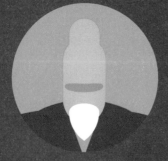

MASTERS: An'ya Kuro, Yoda
APPRENTICES: A'Sharad Hett, Anakin Skywalker, Dama Montalvo, Tarr Seirr

FILM(S)

I   II   III   IV   V   VI

Birth: 896 BBY
Death: 4 ABY
Species: Unknown
Planet: Unknown
♂
66 cm
17 kg

YODA

MASTER: N'Kata Del Gormo
APPRENTICES: Count Dooku, Mace Windu, Cin Drallig, Ikrit, Qu Rahn, Rahm Kota, Obi-Wan Kenobi, Kit Fisto, Ki-Adi-Mundi, Oppo Rancisis, Luke Skywalker

FILM(S)

I   II   III   IV   V   VI

Birth: Unknown
Death: 19 BBY
Species: Iktotchi
Planet: Iktotch
♂
1.88 m

SAESEE TIIN

MASTER: Omo Bouri

FILM(S)

I   II   III   IV   V   VI

Birth: 392 BBY
Death: 19 BBY
Species: Kel Dor
Planet: Kel Dor
♂
1.88 m
80 kg

Birth: Unknown
Death: 27 BBY
Species: Quermian
Planet: Quermia
♂
2.64 m

Birth: 206 BBY
Death: 19 BBY
Species: Thisspiasian
Planet: Thisspias
♂
1.38 m

PLO KOON

MASTER: Tyvokka
APPRENTICES: Bultar Swan, Lissarkh

YARAEL POOF

APPRENTICE: Roron Corobb

OPPO RANCISIS

MASTERS: Yaddle, Yoda

FILM(S)

I II III IV V VI

FILM(S)

I II III IV V VI

FILM(S)

I II III IV V VI

Birth: Unknown
Death: 20 BBY
Species: Tholothian
Planet: Coruscant
♀
1.84 m
50 kg

Birth: 509 BBY
Death: 26 BBY
Species: Unknown
Planet: Unknown
♀
61 cm

Birth: Unknown
Death: 21 BBY
Species: Lannik
Planet: Lannik
♂
1.22 m

ADI GALLIA

APPRENTICE: Siri Tachi

YADDLE

MASTER: Polvin Kut
APPRENTICES: Oppo Rancisis, Empatojayos Brand

EVEN PIELL

APPRENTICE: Jax Pavan

FILM(S)

I II III IV V VI

FILM(S)

I II III IV V VI

FILM(S)

I II III IV V VI

JEDI VS SITH

THE DEADLY STRUGGLE BETWEEN THE SITH AND THE JEDI IS THE FOUNDATION ON WHICH THE *STAR WARS* UNIVERSE IS BUILT. HERE ARE THE MOMENTS WHERE YOU CAN SEE IT HAPPEN BEFORE YOUR VERY EYES.

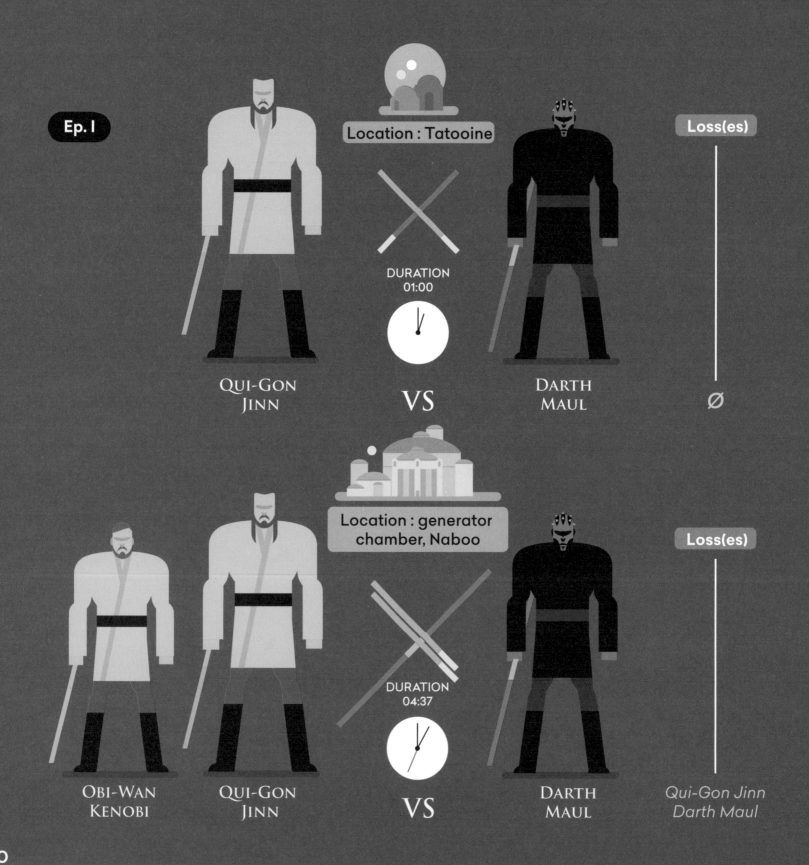

Ep. I

Location : Tatooine

DURATION
01:00

QUI-GON
JINN

VS

DARTH
MAUL

Loss(es)

Ø

Location : generator
chamber, Naboo

DURATION
04:37

OBI-WAN
KENOBI

QUI-GON
JINN

VS

DARTH
MAUL

Loss(es)

Qui-Gon Jinn
Darth Maul

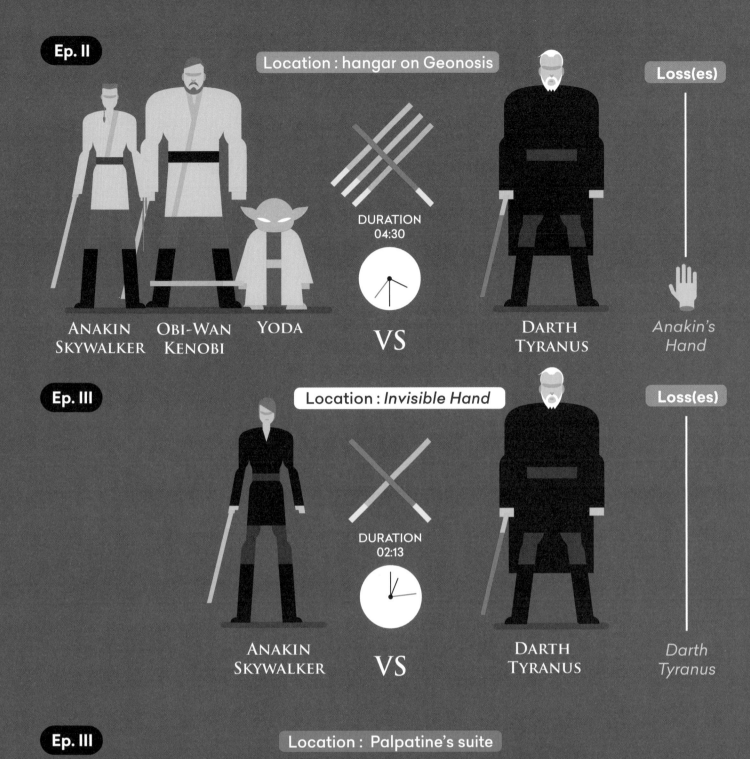

Ep. II

Location : hangar on Geonosis

Loss(es)

DURATION
04:30

ANAKIN
SKYWALKER   OBI-WAN
KENOBI   YODA   VS   DARTH
TYRANUS

*Anakin's
Hand*

Ep. III

Location : *Invisible Hand*

Loss(es)

DURATION
02:13

ANAKIN
SKYWALKER   VS   DARTH
TYRANUS

*Darth
Tyranus*

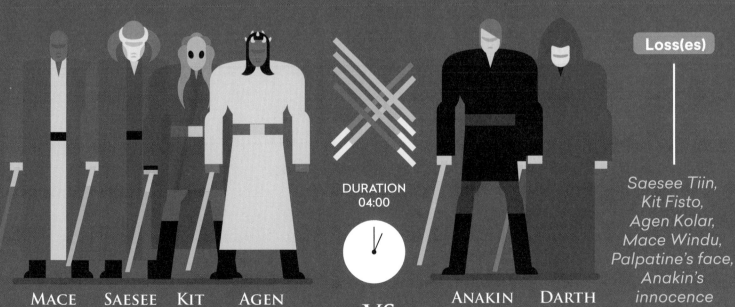

Ep. III

Location : Palpatine's suite

Loss(es)

DURATION
04:00

MACE
WINDU   SAESEE
TIIN   KIT
FISTO   AGEN
KOLAR   VS   ANAKIN
SKYWALKER   DARTH
SIDIOUS

*Saesee Tiin,
Kit Fisto,
Agen Kolar,
Mace Windu,
Palpatine's face,
Anakin's
innocence*

Jedi vs Sith

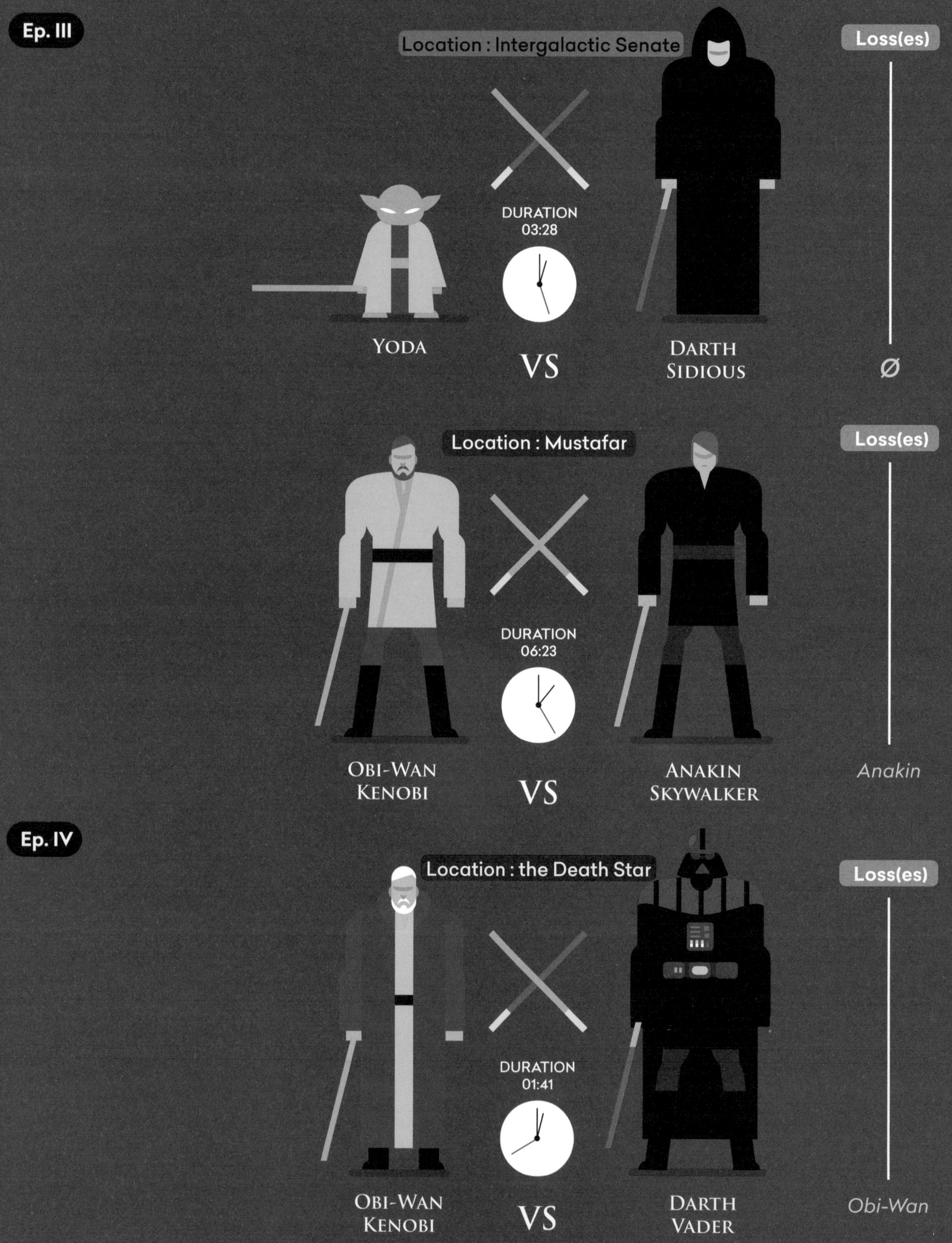

Location : Intergalactic Senate

Loss(es)

DURATION
03:28

YODA

VS

DARTH
SIDIOUS

Ø

Location : Mustafar

Loss(es)

DURATION
06:23

OBI-WAN
KENOBI

VS

ANAKIN
SKYWALKER

Anakin

Location : the Death Star

Loss(es)

DURATION
01:41

OBI-WAN
KENOBI

VS

DARTH
VADER

Obi-Wan

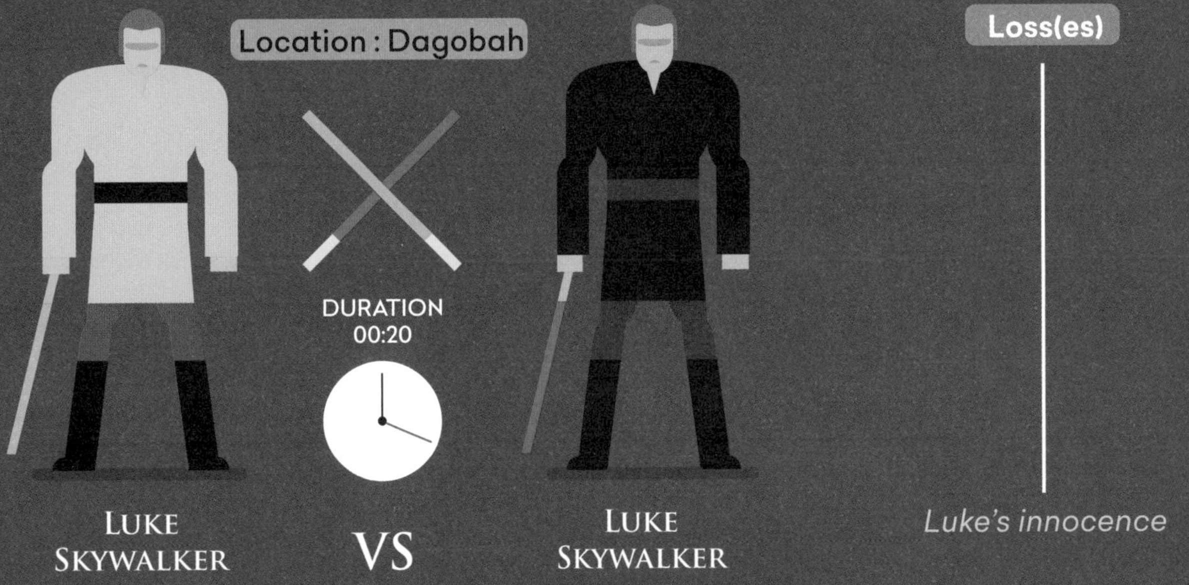

Location : Dagobah

DURATION
00:20

LUKE
SKYWALKER

VS

LUKE
SKYWALKER

Loss(es)

Luke's innocence

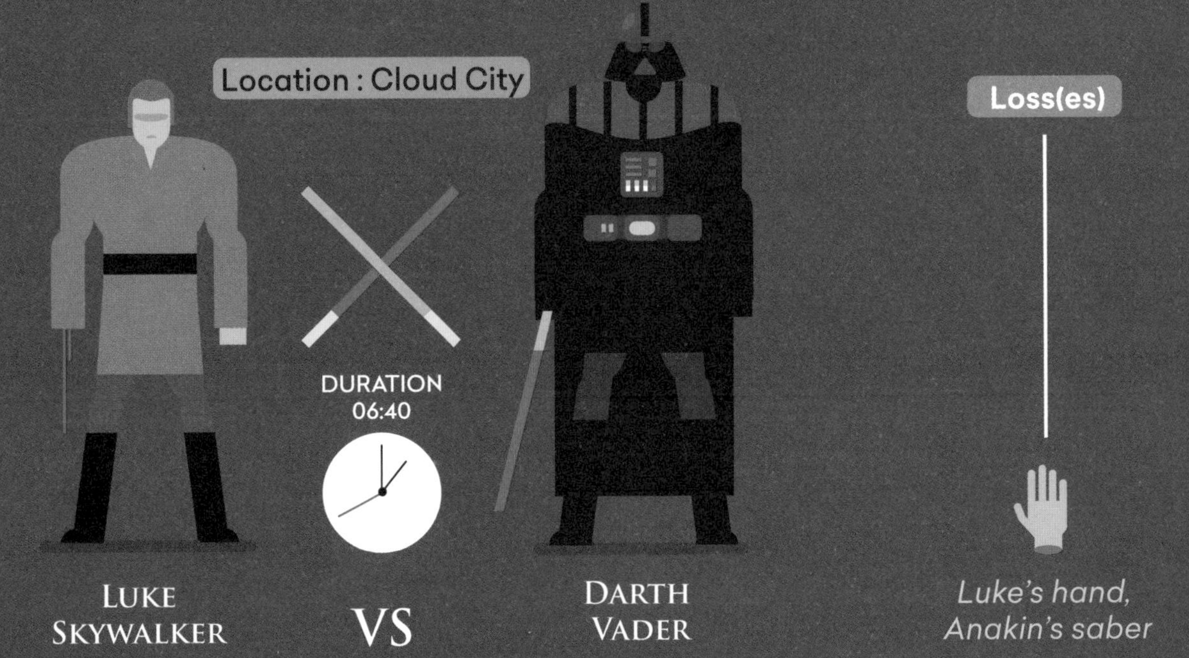

Location : Cloud City

DURATION
06:40

LUKE
SKYWALKER

VS

DARTH
VADER

Loss(es)

*Luke's hand,
Anakin's saber*

Ep. VI

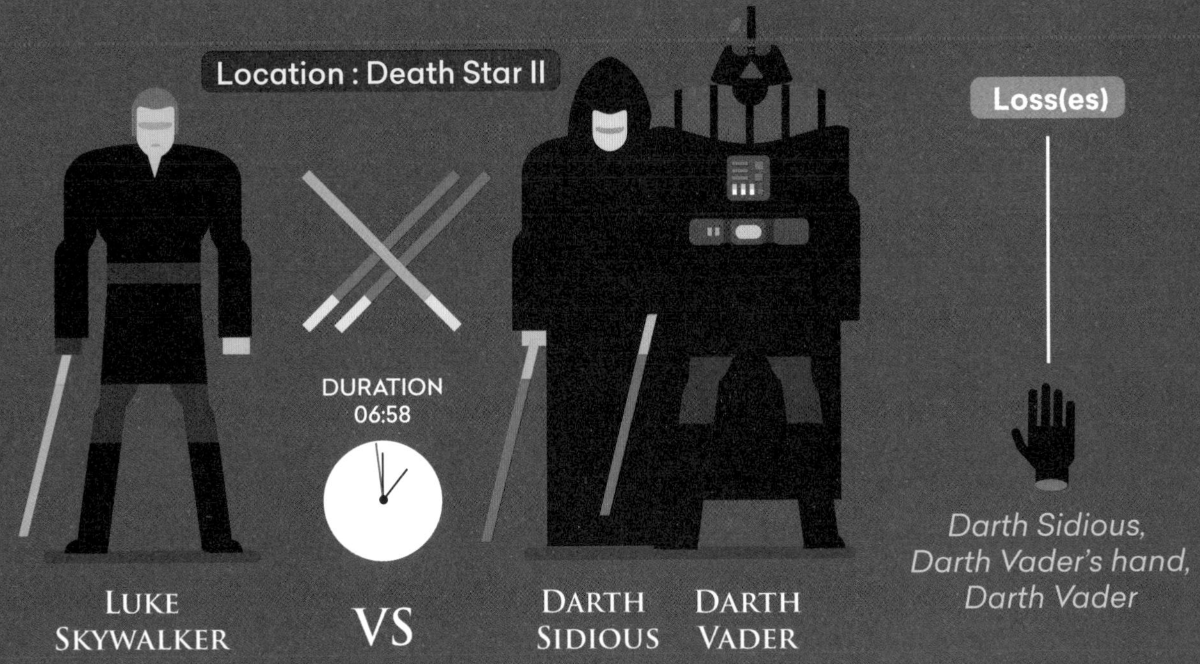

Location : Death Star II

DURATION
06:58

LUKE
SKYWALKER

VS

DARTH
SIDIOUS

DARTH
VADER

Loss(es)

*Darth Sidious,
Darth Vader's hand,
Darth Vader*

EXECUTIONERS AND VICTIMS

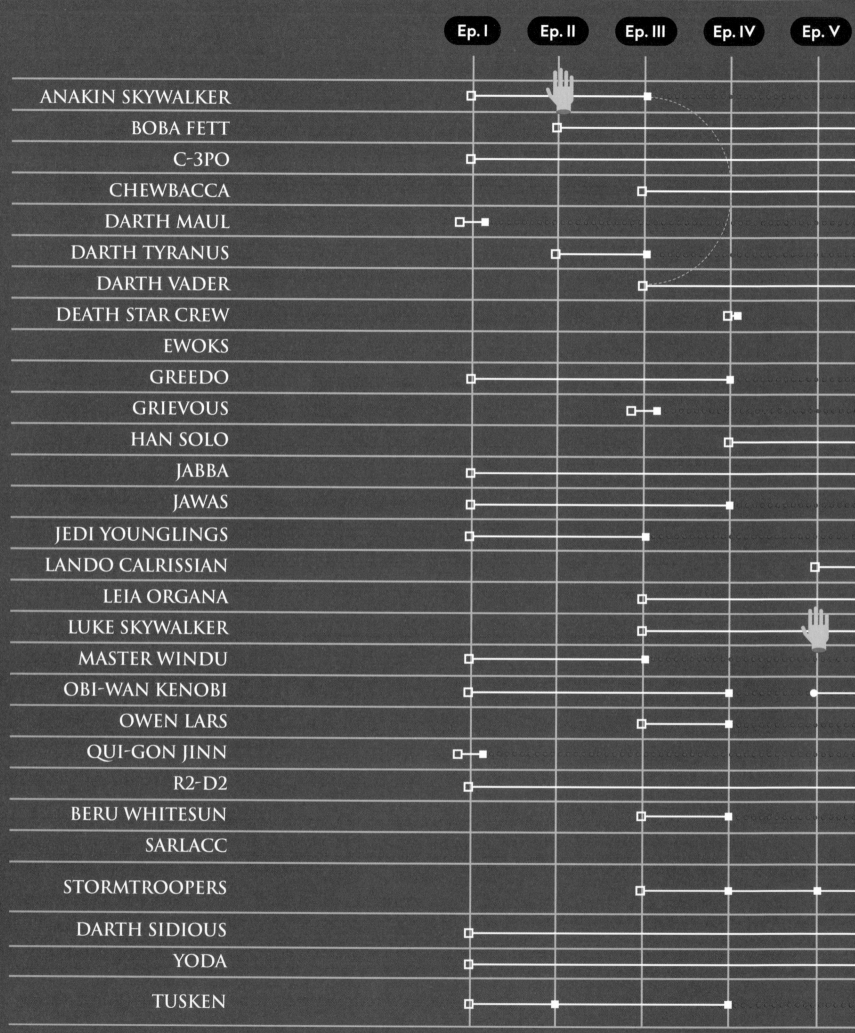

	Ep. I	Ep. II	Ep. III	Ep. IV	Ep. V
ANAKIN SKYWALKER	□		■		
BOBA FETT		□			
C-3PO	□				
CHEWBACCA			□		
DARTH MAUL	□—■				
DARTH TYRANUS		□	■		
DARTH VADER			□		
DEATH STAR CREW				□■	
EWOKS					
GREEDO	□		■		
GRIEVOUS			□—■		
HAN SOLO				□	
JABBA	□				
JAWAS	□			■	
JEDI YOUNGLINGS	□		■		
LANDO CALRISSIAN					□
LEIA ORGANA			□		
LUKE SKYWALKER			□		
MASTER WINDU	□		■		
OBI-WAN KENOBI	□			■	●
OWEN LARS			□	■	
QUI-GON JINN	□—■				
R2-D2	□				
BERU WHITESUN			□	■	
SARLACC					
STORMTROOPERS			□	■	■
DARTH SIDIOUS	□				
YODA	□				
TUSKEN	□	■		■	

24

EXECUTIONERS AND VICTIMS

□——— Appearance
■∙∙∙∙∙∙ Death
●——— Reappearance
▷----⊦ Life

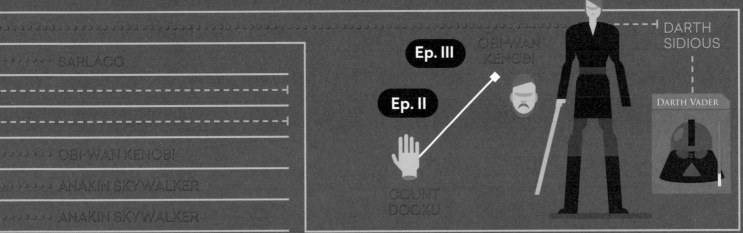

Ep. III

OBI-WAN KENOBI

DARTH SIDIOUS

DARTH VADER

Ep. II

COUNT DOOKU

SARLACC

OBI-WAN KENOBI

ANAKIN SKYWALKER

ANAKIN SKYWALKER

LUKE SKYWALKER / LANDO CALRISSIAN

STORMTROOPERS

HAN SOLO

OBI-WAN KENOBI

LEIA

STORMTROOPERS

ANAKIN SKYWALKER

DARTH SIDIOUS

DARTH VADER

STORMTROOPERS

DARTH MAUL

STORMTROOPERS

DARTH VADER

OLD AGE

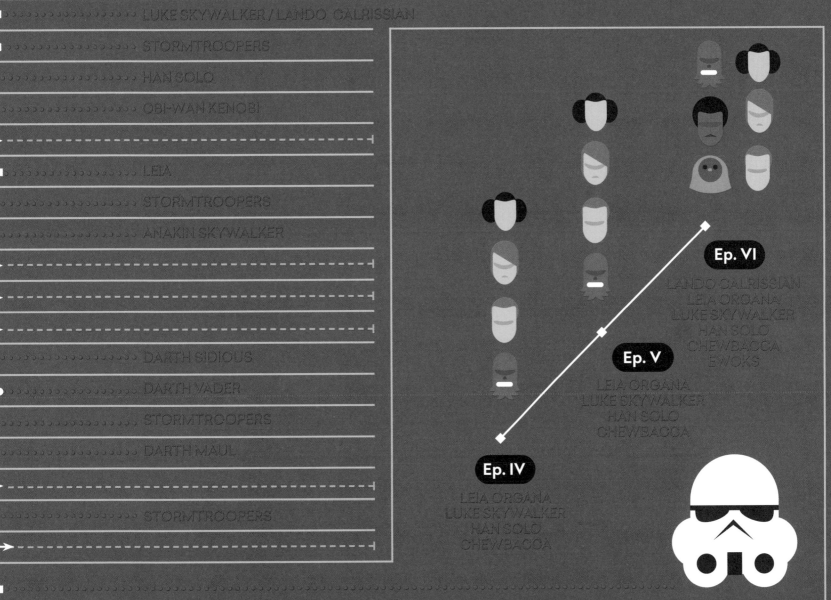

Ep. VI

LANDO CALRISSIAN
LEIA ORGANA
LUKE SKYWALKER
HAN SOLO
CHEWBACCA
EWOKS

Ep. V

LEIA ORGANA
LUKE SKYWALKER
HAN SOLO
CHEWBACCA

Ep. IV

LEIA ORGANA
LUKE SKYWALKER
HAN SOLO
CHEWBACCA

Ep. II   Ep. VI

ANAKIN SKYWALKER STORMTROOPERS

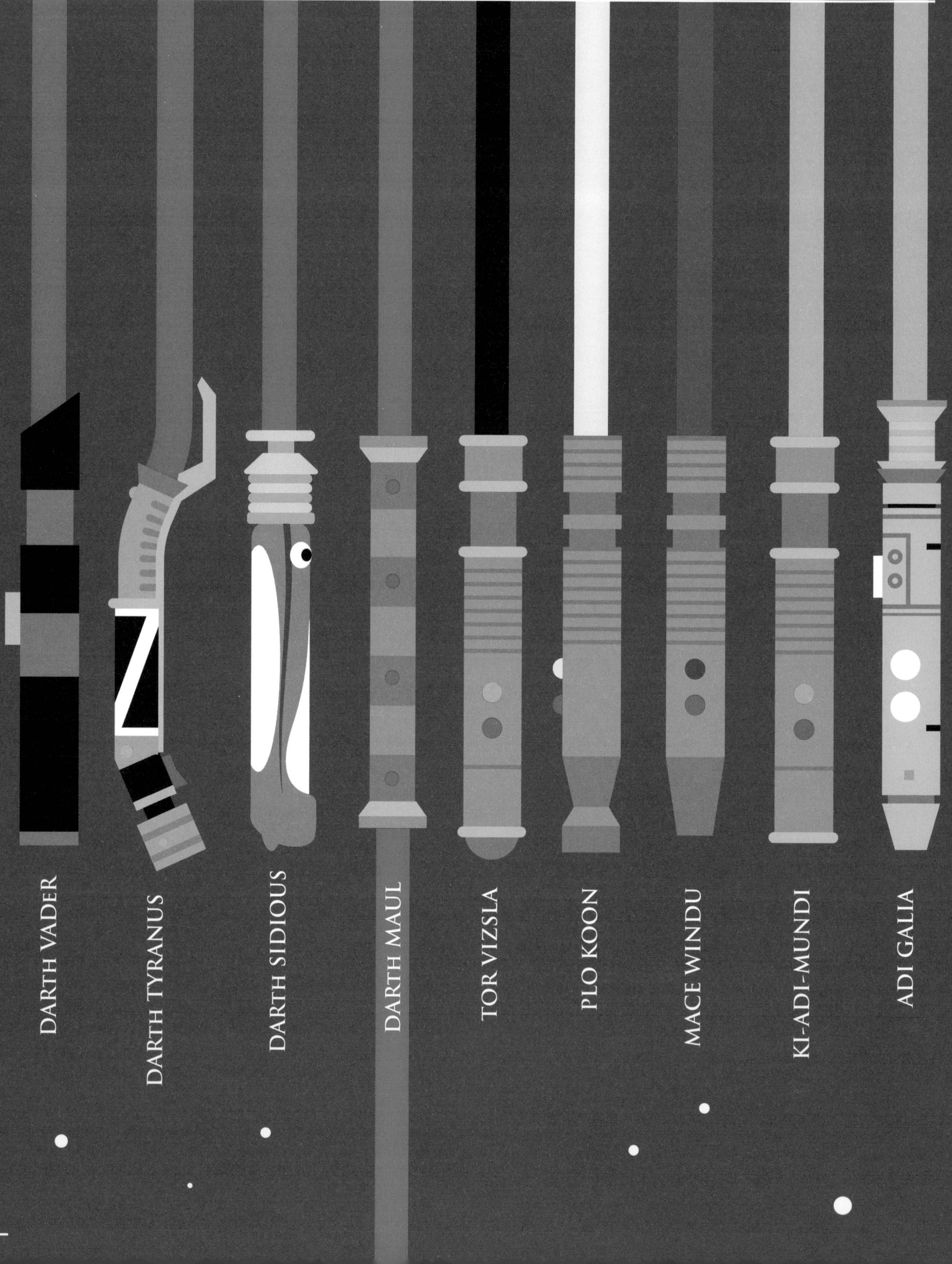

DARTH VADER

DARTH TYRANUS

DARTH SIDIOUS

DARTH MAUL

TOR VIZSLA

PLO KOON

MACE WINDU

KI-ADI-MUNDI

ADI GALLIA

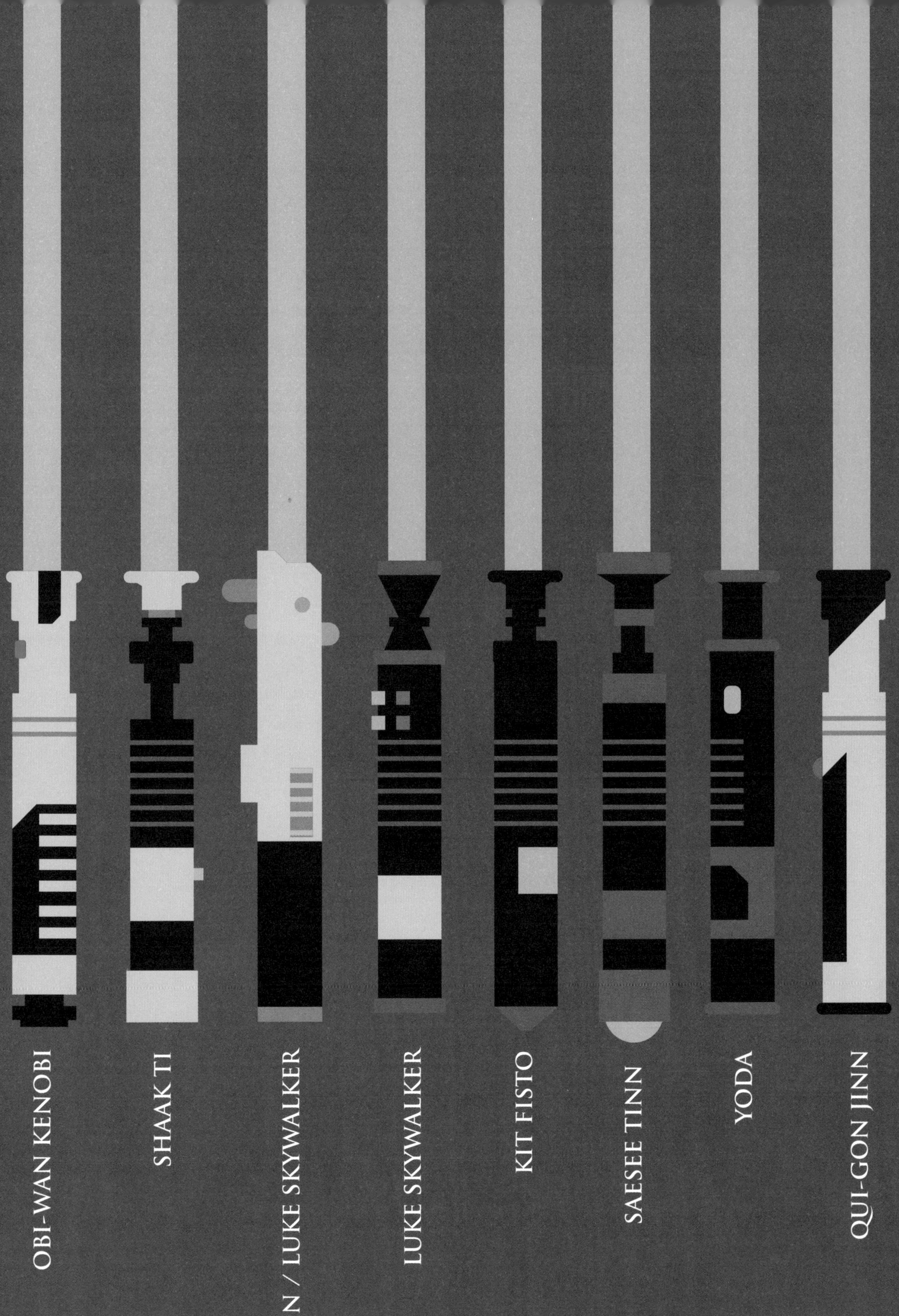

OBI-WAN KENOBI

SHAAK TI

ANAKIN / LUKE SKYWALKER

LUKE SKYWALKER

KIT FISTO

SAESEE TINN

YODA

QUI-GON JINN

Classification of Vessels According to their Speed

Platoon Attack Craft
FEDERATION — I

112 B1 droids, or 20 droidekas

50 Km/h

500 Km/h

74-A SPEEDER BIKE
EMPIRE — VI

AX-20m blaster cannon

250 Km/h LANDSPEEDER
NEUTRAL — IV

50 100 150 200 250 300 350 400 450

80 Km/h

OG-9 HOMING SPIDER DROID
FEDERATION — II

Mounted laser rifle
• Antipersonnel laser cannon
• Retractable ion cannon

60 Km/h

AT-AT
EMPIRE — V / VI

2 Taim & Bak MS-1 laser cannons
• 2 FF-4 repeating blasters
• Durasteel/Transport footpads
• 5 speeder bikes, 2 AT-ST/40 troopers

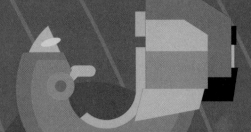

A/SF-01 B-WING
Rebellion
VI

950 Km/h

NABOO ROYAL STARSHIP
Republic — I / II / III

920 Km/h

3 ArMek SW-7a light ion cannons
• 1 Gyrhill R-9X heavy laser cannon
• 1 Gyrhill 72 double autoblaster
• 2 Krupx MG9 proton torpedo launchers, armed with 8 torpedoes each

650 Km/h

BLOOD FIN
Empire — I

550	600	650	700	750	800	850	900	950	1 000	Km/h

STAR DESTROYER
Empire — IV / V / VI

975 Km/h

TIE BOMBER
Empire — IV / V / VI

850 Km/h

• 2 L-s1 laser cannons
• 2 SFS T-s5 torpedo launchers (4 torpedoes)
• 2 SFS M-s3 concussion missile launchers (8 missiles)
• 1 hold containing ArmaTek SJ-62/68 orbital mines
• ArmaTek VL-61/79 proton bombs
• Thermal detonators

• 6 dual heavy turbolaser cannon turrets
• 2 dual ion cannon turrets
• 4 turbolasers
• 5 medium turbolasers
• 60 Taim & Bak XX-9 turbolasers
• 60 Borstel NK-7 ion cannons
• 10 Phylon Q7 tractor beam projectors
• 48 TIE fighters
• 12 TIE bombers
• 12 TIE transports
• 8 Lambda transport shuttles
• 15 Delta transports
• 5 assault ships
• 1 Gamma assault shuttle
• Maintenance vehicles
• AT-AT Theta barges
• 12 Sentinel transports
• 20 AT-AT, 30 AT-ST/9,235 officers
• 9700 troopers
• 27,850 reserves
• 275 gunners

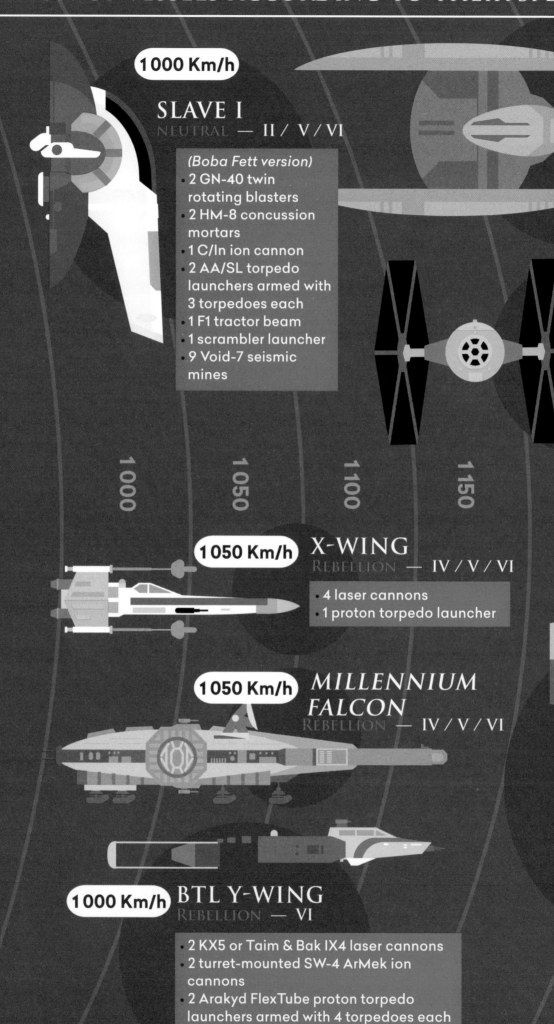

1 000 Km/h

SLAVE I
NEUTRAL — II / V / VI

(Boba Fett version)
• 2 GN-40 twin rotating blasters
• 2 HM-8 concussion mortars
• 1 C/In ion cannon
• 2 AA/SL torpedo launchers armed with 3 torpedoes each
• 1 F1 tractor beam
• 1 scrambler launcher
• 9 Void-7 seismic mines

1 200 Km/h

VULTURE DROID STARFIGHT
FEDERATION — I /

• 6 blaster cannons
• 2 energy torpedo lo

1 200 Km/h

TIE FIGHTE
EMPIRE — IV / V

• 2 laser cannons

1000   1050   1100   1150   1200   1250

1 050 Km/h

X-WING
REBELLION — IV / V / VI

• 4 laser cannons
• 1 proton torpedo launcher

1 050 Km/h

MILLENNIUM FALCON
REBELLION — IV / V / VI

1 200 Km/h

ACCLAMATO
TRANSGALAC
REPUBLIC — II

• 12 quadruple turbolas cannons
• 24 laser cannons
• 4 proton mortars
• 16,000 clone troopers + crew

1 000 Km/h

BTL Y-WING
REBELLION — VI

• 2 KX5 or Taim & Bak IX4 laser cannons
• 2 turret-mounted SW-4 ArMek ion cannons
• 2 Arakyd FlexTube proton torpedo launchers armed with 4 torpedoes each
• Proton bombs

RZ1 A-WING
Rebellion — IV / V / VI

1 300 Km/h

- 2 Borstel RG-9 laser cannons
- 2 Dymek HM-6 concussion missile launchers armed with 6 missiles each

COUNT DOOKU'S SOLAR SAILER
Federation — II

1 600 Km/h

- 84 tractor/repulsor beams

1300   1350   1400   1450   1500   1550   1600   Km/h

...ASS
TRANSPORT

DELTA-7 AETHERSPRITE LIGHT INTERCEPTOR
Republic — III

1 500 Km/h

- 2 laser cannons
- 2 ion cannons

E-WING
Republic — I / II / III

1 300 Km/h

- 3 laser cannons
- 1 proton torpedo launcher
- 16 torpedoes

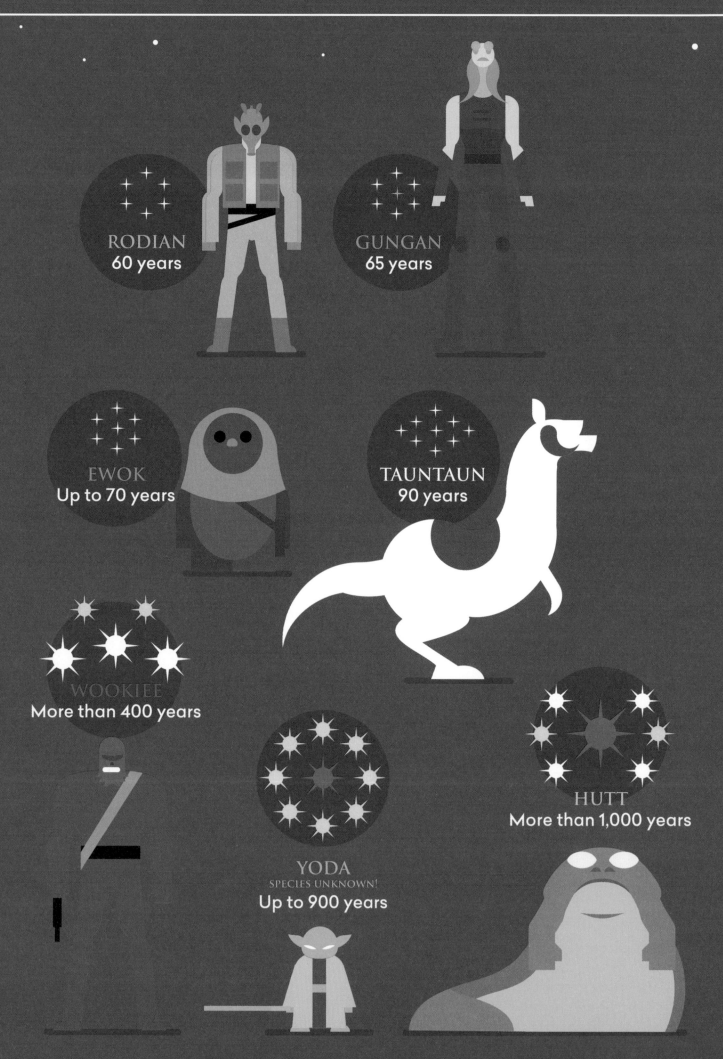

RODIAN
60 years

GUNGAN
65 years

EWOK
Up to 70 years

TAUNTAUN
90 years

WOOKIEE
More than 400 years

HUTT
More than 1,000 years

YODA
SPECIES UNKNOWN!
Up to 900 years

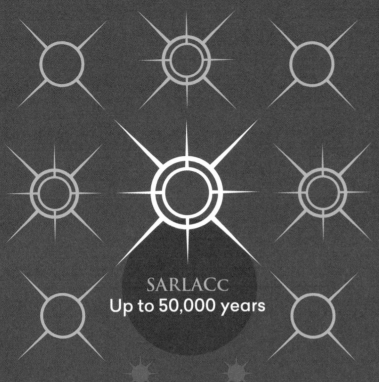

SARLACC
Up to 50,000 years

LIFE EXPECTANCY IN THE GALAXY FAR, FAR AWAY

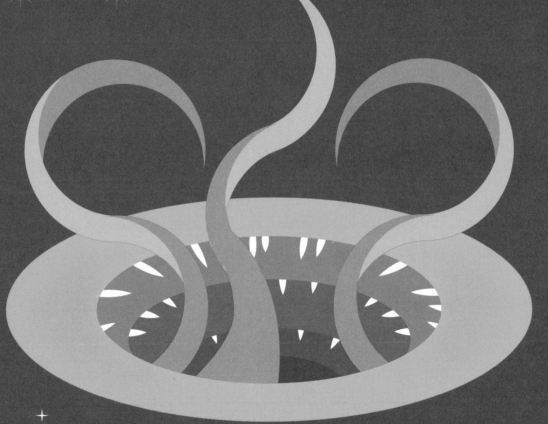

5 years

10 years

50 years

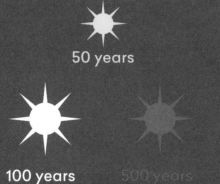

100 years

500 years

1,000 years

10,000 years

15,000 years

LOVE IN THE STARS

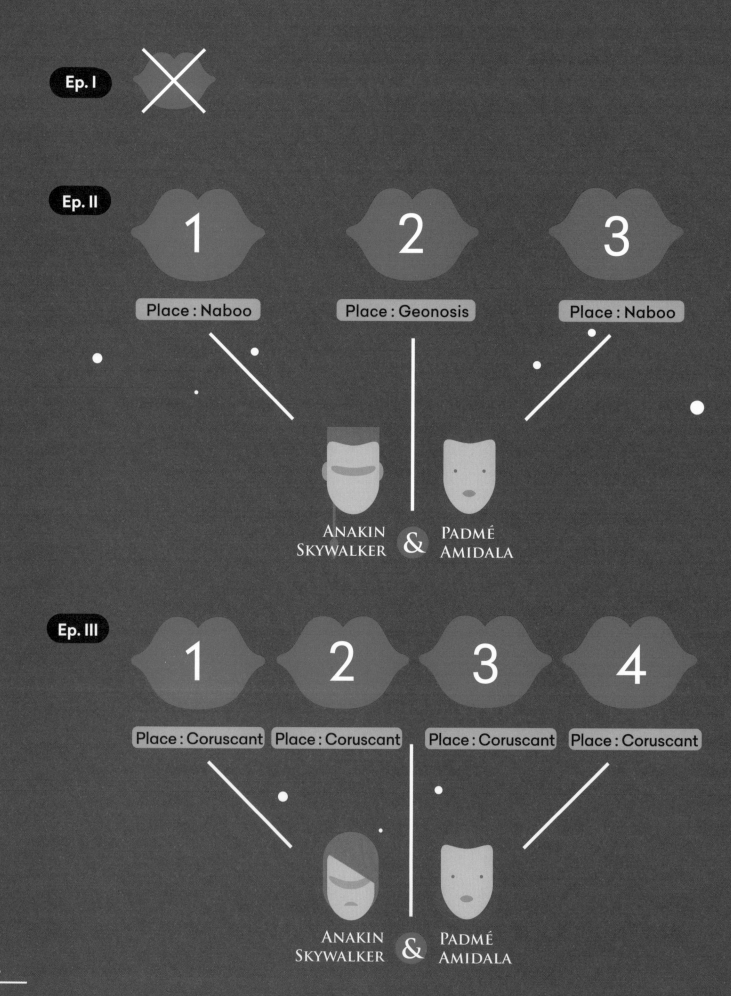

Ep. I

Ep. II

1 — Place : Naboo
2 — Place : Geonosis
3 — Place : Naboo

ANAKIN SKYWALKER & PADMÉ AMIDALA

Ep. III

1 — Place : Coruscant
2 — Place : Coruscant
3 — Place : Coruscant
4 — Place : Coruscant

ANAKIN SKYWALKER & PADMÉ AMIDALA

Ep. IV

Ep. V

1 — Place : Hoth

2 — Place : *Falcon*

3 — Place : Bespin

LUKE SKYWALKER & LEIA ORGANA

HAN SOLO & LEIA ORGANA

Ep. VI

1 — Place : Tatooine

2 — Place : Endor

3 — Place : Endor

4 — Place : Endor

HAN SOLO & LEIA ORGANA

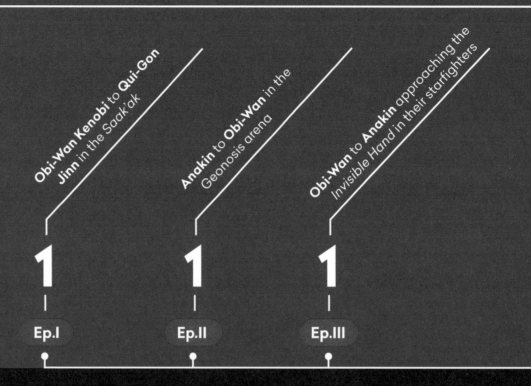

Obi-Wan Kenobi to **Qui-Gon Jinn** in the *Saak'ak*

1

Ep.I

Anakin to **Obi-Wan** in the Geonosis arena

1

Ep.II

Obi-Wan to **Anakin** approaching the *Invisible Hand* in their starfighters

1

Ep.III

'I HAVE A BAD FEELING ABOUT THIS'

8 V

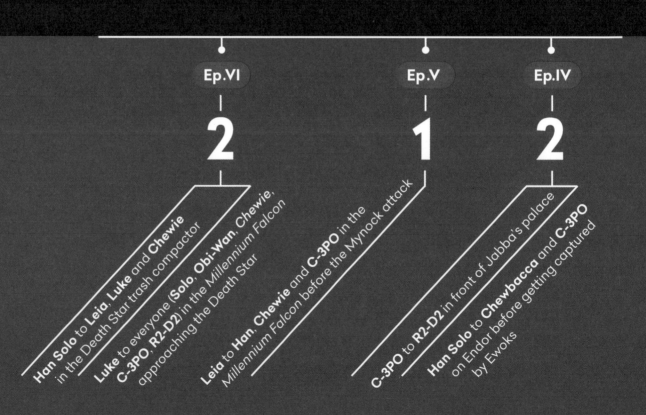

Ep.VI

2

Han Solo to **Leia**, **Luke** and **Chewie** in the Death Star trash compactor

Luke to everyone (**Solo**, **Obi-Wan**, **Chewie**, **C-3PO**, **R2-D2**) in the *Millennium Falcon* approaching the Death Star

Ep.V

1

Leia to **Han**, **Chewie** and **C-3PO** in the *Millennium Falcon* before the Mynock attack

Ep.IV

2

C-3PO to **R2-D2** in front of Jabba's palace

Han Solo to **Chewbacca** and **C-3PO** on Endor before getting captured by Ewoks

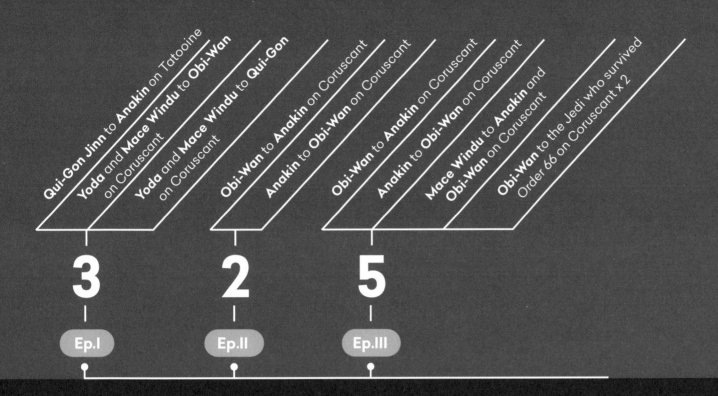

Qui-Gon Jinn to **Anakin** on Tatooine

Yoda and **Mace Windu** to **Obi-Wan** on Coruscant

Yoda and **Mace Windu** to **Qui-Gon** on Coruscant

Obi-Wan to **Anakin** on Coruscant

Anakin to **Obi-Wan** on Coruscant

Obi-Wan to **Anakin** on Coruscant

Anakin to **Obi-Wan** on Coruscant

Mace Windu to **Anakin** and **Obi-Wan** on Coruscant

Obi-Wan to the Jedi who survived Order 66 on Coruscant x 2

3

2

5

Ep.I

Ep.II

Ep.III

$14 'MAY THE FORCE BE WITH YOU'

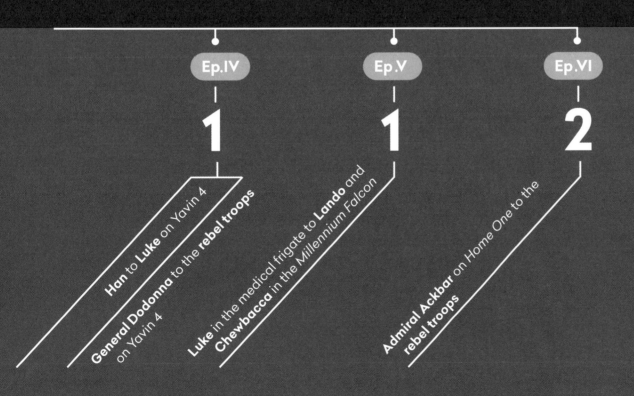

Ep.IV

Ep.V

Ep.VI

1

1

2

Han to **Luke** on Yavin 4

General Dodonna to the **rebel troops** on Yavin 4

Luke in the medical frigate to **Lando** and **Chewbacca** in the *Millennium Falcon*

Admiral Ackbar on *Home One* to the **rebel troops**

Body parts lost in *Star Wars*

A lot of characters lose body parts in the Star Wars story.
Humans, aliens, droids, Jedi, Siths – be it intended or unintended
– all are at risk.

Ep. I DARTH MAUL
ABDOMEN
by Obi-Wan Kenobi

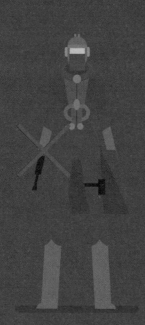

Ep. II ZAM WESELL
RIGHT HAND
by Obi-Wan Kenobi

Ep. II JANGO FETT
HEAD
by Mace Windu

Ep. III COUNT DOOKU
HANDS AND HEAD
by Anakin Skywalker

C-3PO

Ep. II HEAD
by a factory robot

Ep. IV RIGHT ARM
by a Tusken Raider

Ep. V ALL HIS LIMBS

Ep. VI AN EYE
by Salacious Crumb

Ep. II ACKLAY
2 OF ITS 6 CLAWS
by Obi-Wan Kenobi

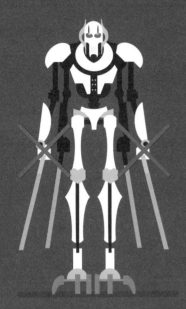

Ep. III GENERAL GRIEVOUS
2 OF 4 HANDS

by Obi-Wan Kenobi

Ep. III MACE WINDU
RIGHT HAND

by Anakin Skywalker

Ep. III CLONE TROOPERS
2 HEADS AND 1 RIGHT ARM

by Yoda

Ep. VI DARTH VADER
RIGHT HAND
by Luke Skywalker

Ep. V WAMPA
RIGHT ARM
by Luke Skywalker

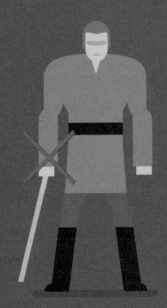

Ep. V LUKE SKYWALKER
RIGHT HAND

by Darth Vader

ANAKIN SKYWALKER
RIGHT FOREARM

Ep. II
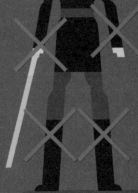

by Count Dooku

Ep. III

LEGS AND LEFT FOREARM
by Obi-Wan Kenobi

A LONG TIME AGO IN A GALAXY FAR, FAR AWAY, THERE WAS A PHRASE, A TITLE AND A FEW INTRODUCTIONS.

LINES   WORDS   LETTERS   PARAGRAPHS   SENTENCES   ADJECTIVES   NOUNS   VERBS

Ep.I THE PHANTOM MENACE

FIRST WORDS:
TURMOIL HAS ENGULFED

LAST WORDS:
SETTLE THE CONFLICT

LINES	WORDS	LETTERS	PARAGRAPHS	SENTENCES	ADJECTIVES	NOUNS	VERBS
18	78	489	3	4	10	24	7

Ep.II ATTACK OF THE CLONES

FIRST WORDS:
THERE IS UNREST

LAST WORDS:
THE OVERWHELMED JEDI

LINES	WORDS	LETTERS	PARAGRAPHS	SENTENCES	ADJECTIVES	NOUNS	VERBS
18	80	487	3	4	10	20	9

Ep.III REVENGE OF THE SITH

FIRST WORDS:
WAR!

LAST WORDS :
THE CAPTIVE CHANCELLOR

LINES	WORDS	LETTERS	PARAGRAPHS	SENTENCES	ADJECTIVES	NOUNS	VERBS
17	75	479	3	6	12	21	9

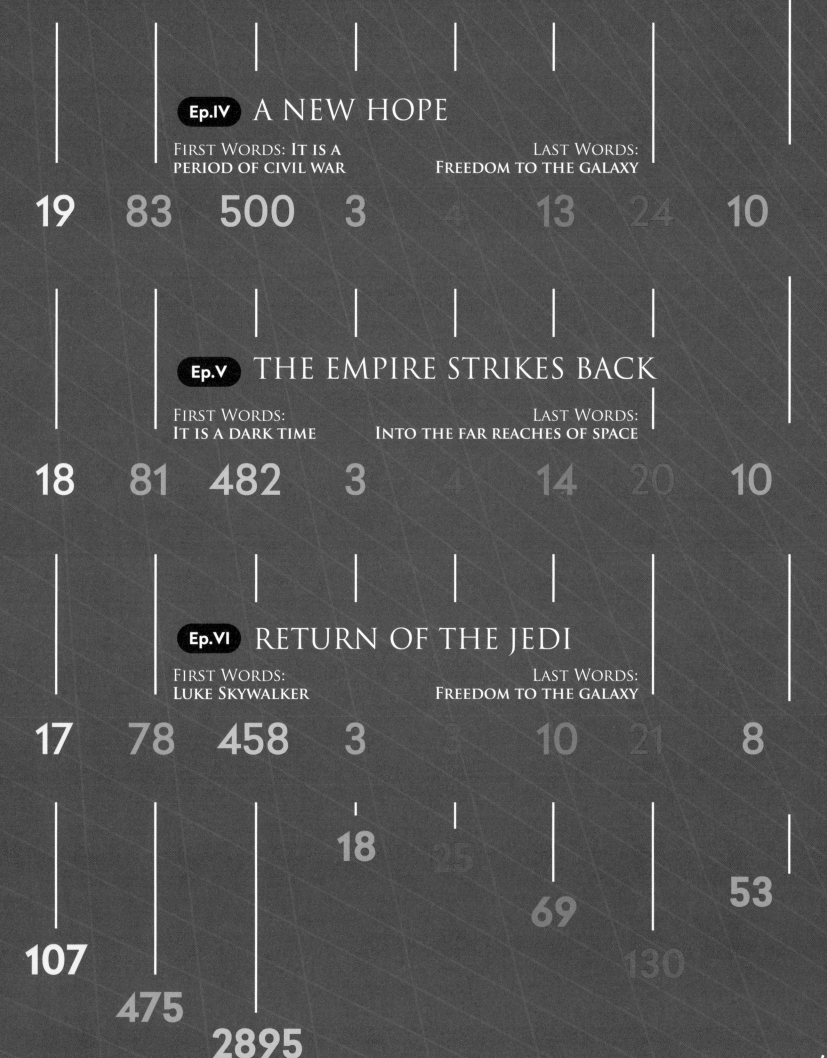

Ep.IV A NEW HOPE

FIRST WORDS: IT IS A
PERIOD OF CIVIL WAR

LAST WORDS:
FREEDOM TO THE GALAXY

19 83 **500** 3 4 **13** 24 **10**

Ep.V THE EMPIRE STRIKES BACK

FIRST WORDS:
IT IS A DARK TIME

LAST WORDS:
INTO THE FAR REACHES OF SPACE

18 81 **482** 3 4 **14** 20 **10**

Ep.VI RETURN OF THE JEDI

FIRST WORDS:
LUKE SKYWALKER

LAST WORDS:
FREEDOM TO THE GALAXY

17 78 **458** 3 3 **10** 21 **8**

18

25

69

53

107

130

475

2895

A BRIEF HISTORY OF TIME

4 CARTOONS 1985-2014

6 FILMS 1977-2005

92 VIDEO GAMES 1999-2010

115 COMICS 1977-2015

307 BOOKS 1991-2012

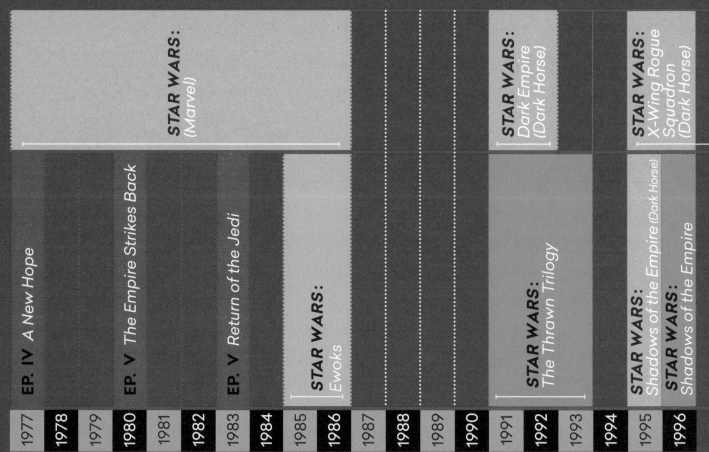

STAR WARS: (Marvel)

STAR WARS: Dark Empire (Dark Horse)

STAR WARS: X-Wing Rogue Squadron (Dark Horse)

EP. IV A New Hope

EP. V The Empire Strikes Back

EP. V Return of the Jedi

STAR WARS: Ewoks

STAR WARS: The Thrawn Trilogy

STAR WARS: Shadows of the Empire (Dark Horse)

STAR WARS: Shadows of the Empire

| 1977 | 1978 | 1979 | 1980 | 1981 | 1982 | 1983 | 1984 | 1985 | 1986 | 1987 | 1988 | 1989 | 1990 | 1991 | 1992 | 1993 | 1994 | 1995 | 1996 |

STAR WARS:
X-Wing Rogue
Squadron
(Dark Horse)

STAR WARS:
Episode I : Racer

STAR WARS:
Knights of the Old Republic II

STAR WARS:
Labyrinth of Evil

STAR WARS:
Rogue Squadron II: Rogue Leader

STAR WARS:
Knights of the Old Republic

STAR WARS:
Lego Star Wars: The Video Game

STAR WARS:
The Force Unleashed

STAR WARS:
The Force Unleashed II

STAR WARS:
The Han Solo Trilogy

EP. I The Phantom Menace

STAR WARS:
Tag & Bink are Dead (Dark Horse)

EP. II Attack of the Clones

STAR WARS:
Galaxies

STAR WARS:
The Clone wars

EP. III Revenge of the Sith

STAR WARS:
Darth Plagueis

STAR WARS:
Rebels

STAR WARS:
The Clone Wars

STAR WARS:
(Marvel)

1997
1998
1999
2000
2001
2002
2003
2004
2005
2006
2007
2008
2009
2010
2011
2012
2013
2014
2015

TRILOGIES I & II

U.S.A.

TATOOINE
ENDOR
EP. IV/VI

Death Valley
Redwood
Yuma Desert

SPAIN

NABOO
EP. II

Seville

UNITED KINGDOM

INTERIORS
EP. I/II/III/
IV/V/VI

Elstree Studios
Shepperton Studios
Leavesden Studios
Ealing Studios

TUNISIA

TATOOINE
EP. I/II/IV

Ksar Hadada
Ksar Ouled Soltane
Onk Jemal
Matmata
Chott El Djerid
The Great Dune
Ajim
Sidi Jemour
Shubiel Gorge
Sidi Bouhlel

GUATEMALA

YAVIN 4
EP. IV

Tikal

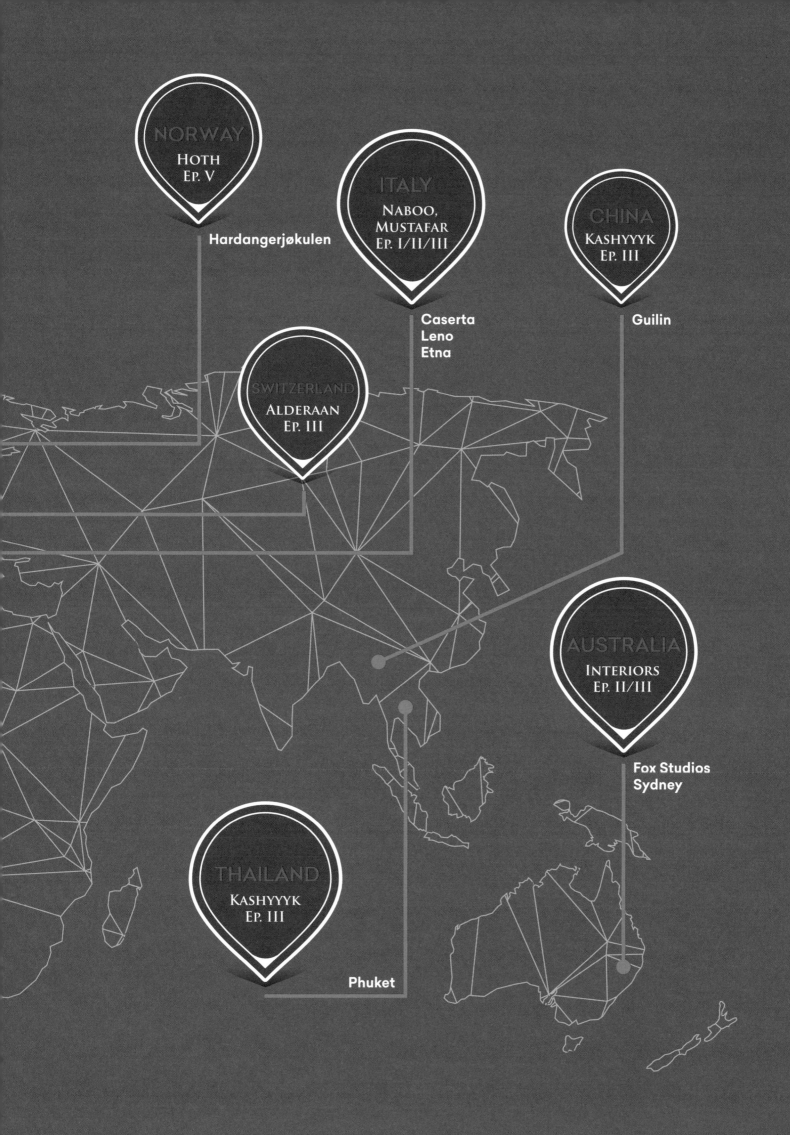

NORWAY
HOTH
EP. V

Hardangerjøkulen

ITALY
NABOO,
MUSTAFAR
EP. I/II/III

Caserta
Leno
Etna

CHINA
KASHYYYK
EP. III

Guilin

SWITZERLAND
ALDERAAN
EP. III

AUSTRALIA
INTERIORS
EP. II/III

Fox Studios
Sydney

THAILAND
KASHYYYK
EP. III

Phuket

It only took a few lines for Boba Fett to become one of the most popular characters in the galaxy. And the rest?

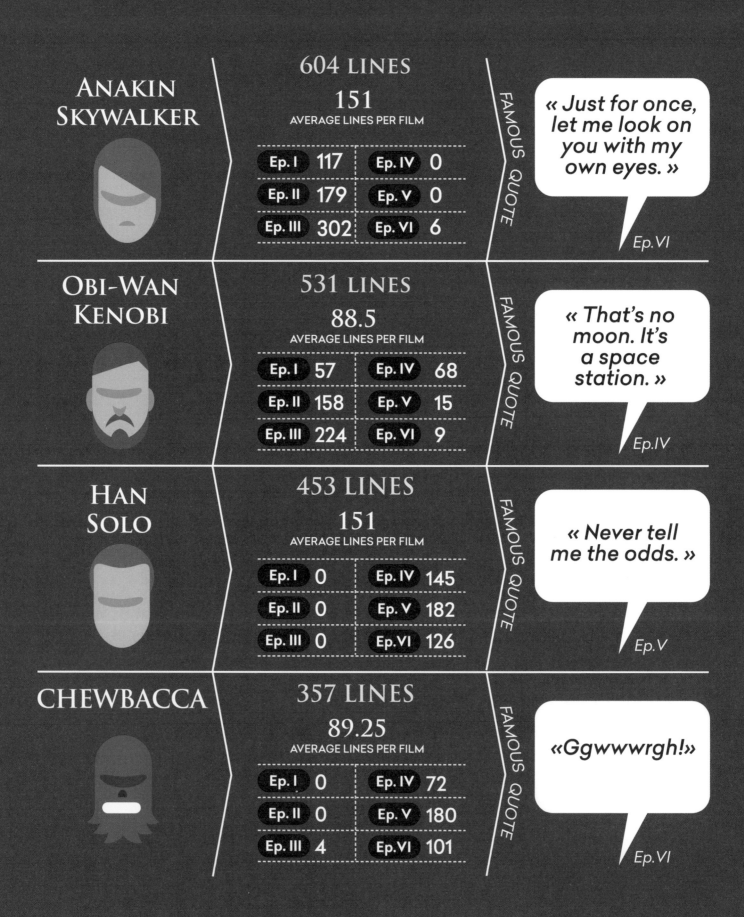

Anakin Skywalker

604 LINES

151
AVERAGE LINES PER FILM

Ep. I	117	Ep. IV	0
Ep. II	179	Ep. V	0
Ep. III	302	Ep. VI	6

FAMOUS QUOTE

« Just for once, let me look on you with my own eyes. »

Ep. VI

Obi-Wan Kenobi

531 LINES

88.5
AVERAGE LINES PER FILM

Ep. I	57	Ep. IV	68
Ep. II	158	Ep. V	15
Ep. III	224	Ep. VI	9

FAMOUS QUOTE

« That's no moon. It's a space station. »

Ep. IV

Han Solo

453 LINES

151
AVERAGE LINES PER FILM

Ep. I	0	Ep. IV	145
Ep. II	0	Ep. V	182
Ep. III	0	Ep. VI	126

FAMOUS QUOTE

« Never tell me the odds. »

Ep. V

Chewbacca

357 LINES

89.25
AVERAGE LINES PER FILM

Ep. I	0	Ep. IV	72
Ep. II	0	Ep. V	180
Ep. III	4	Ep. VI	101

FAMOUS QUOTE

«Ggwwwrgh!»

Ep. VI

R2-D2

249 LINES

41.5
AVERAGE LINES PER FILM

Ep. I	46	Ep. IV	62
Ep. II	17	Ep. V	55
Ep. III	36	Ep. VI	33

FAMOUS QUOTE

« Beep chirp boop whistle. »

Ep. V

YODA

168 LINES

33.6
AVERAGE LINES PER FILM

Ep. I	18	Ep. IV	0
Ep. II	26	Ep. V	58
Ep. III	53	Ep. VI	13

FAMOUS QUOTE

« Do, or do not. There is no try. »

Ep. V

DARTH VADER

146 LINES

36.5
AVERAGE LINES PER FILM

Ep. I	0	Ep. IV	44
Ep. II	0	Ep. V	5§
Ep. III	6	Ep. VI	40

FAMOUS QUOTE

« I am your father. »

Ep. V

JAR JAR BINKS

101 LINES

33.6
AVERAGE LINES PER FILM

Ep. I	87	Ep. IV	0
Ep. II	12	Ep. V	0
Ep. III	2	Ep. VI	0

FAMOUS QUOTE

« Meesa cause mebbe one-a, two-y little bitty accidenties, huh? Yud say boom de gassa, den crashin deh boss's heyblibber, den banished. »

Ep. I

MACE WINDU

79 LINES

26.3
AVERAGE LINES PER FILM

Ep. I	13	Ep. IV	0
Ep. II	30	Ep. V	0
Ep. III	36	Ep. VI	0

FAMOUS QUOTE

« This party's over. »

Ep. II

HOW QUICKLY COULD YOU GET AROUND THE WORLD IN THE *MILLENNIUM FALCON* IF THE HYPERDRIVE WAS BROKEN?

366 H

38.1 H

17.6 H

9.2 H

5.5 H

4 H

48 MIN

2 MIN

LONDON-MOON

AROUND THE WORLD

LONDON-AUCKLAND

LONDON-TOKYO

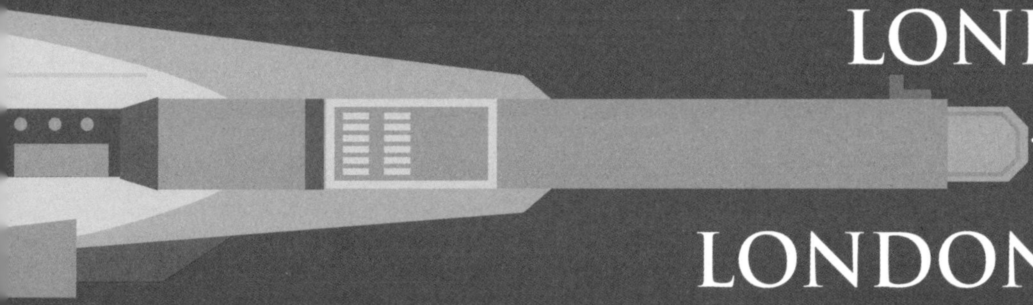

LONDON-NEW YORK

LONDON-DELHI

LONDON-ORKNEY

AROUND THE M-25

CHARACTERS WITH THE MOST ACTION FIGURES

Luke Skywalker

106

(1978–2014)

Obi-Wan Kenobi

84

(1978–2014)

Anakin Skywalker

72

(1985–2014)

Darth Vader

65

(1978–2014)

Han Solo

65

(1978–2014)

Leia Organa

46

(1978–2013)

R2-D2

43

(1978–2013)

Boba Fett

41

(1979–2014)

Yoda

39

(1980–2014)

DARTH MAUL

32

(1999–2014)

PALPATINE

32

(1984–2014)

CHEWBACCA

31

(1978–2014)

STORMTROOPER

28

(1978–2014)

C-3PO

27

(1978–2014)

PADMÉ AMIDALA

26

(1999–2013

MACE WINDU

21

(1998–2013)

LANDO CALRISSIAN

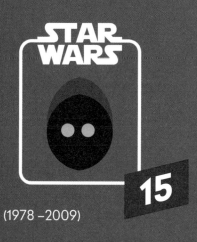

20

(1980–2015)

JAWA

15

(1978 –2009)

GREEDO

(1978–2014)

7

JABBA

(1983–2010)

7

SALACIOUS CRUMB

(1984–2010)

4

2010 · · · · · · · · · · · · ◄ **280**

2000 ———————————

1990 · · · · · · · · · · · · · ◄ **260**

1980 —— ◄ **75**

1970 — ◄ **21**

810

STAR WARS

NUMBER
OF FIGURES
PRODUCED
BY DECADE

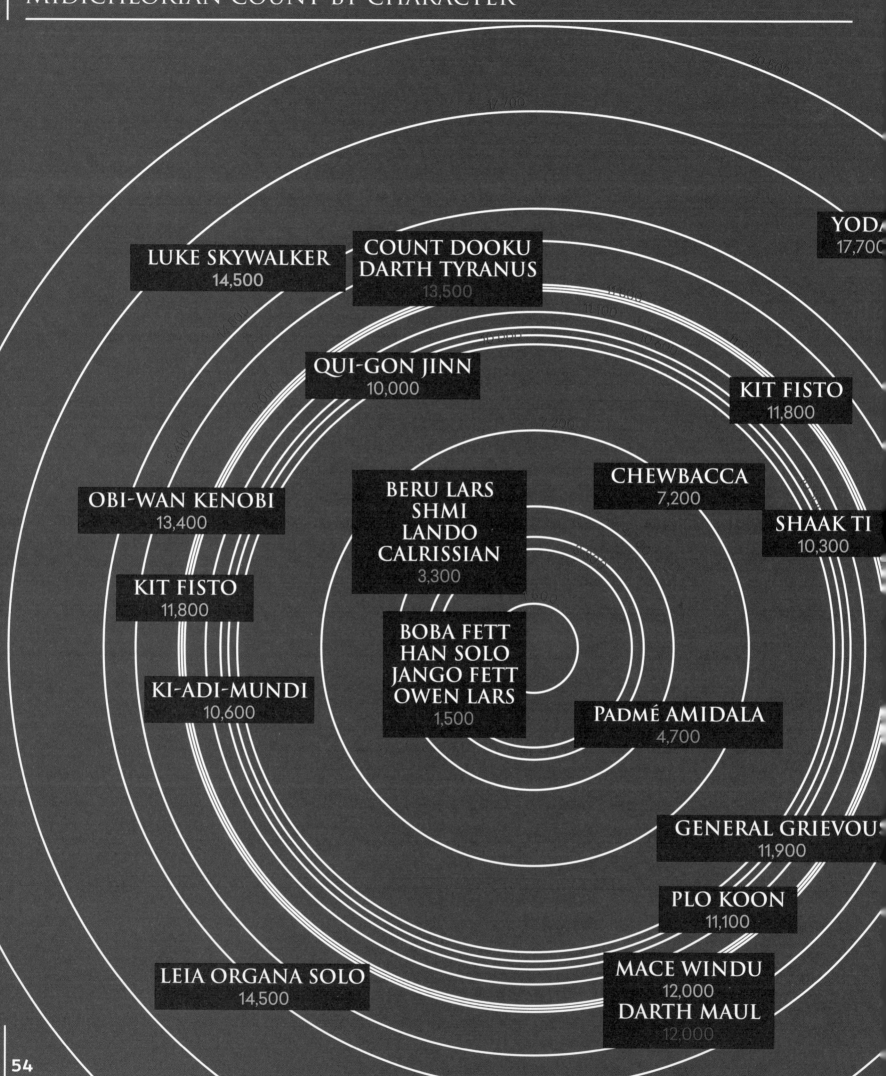

YODA
17,700

LUKE SKYWALKER
14,500

COUNT DOOKU
DARTH TYRANUS
13,500

QUI-GON JINN
10,000

KIT FISTO
11,800

CHEWBACCA
7,200

OBI-WAN KENOBI
13,400

BERU LARS
SHMI
LANDO
CALRISSIAN
3,300

SHAAK TI
10,300

KIT FISTO
11,800

BOBA FETT
HAN SOLO
JANGO FETT
OWEN LARS
1,500

KI-ADI-MUNDI
10,600

PADMÉ AMIDALA
4,700

GENERAL GRIEVOUS
11,900

PLO KOON
11,100

LEIA ORGANA SOLO
14,500

MACE WINDU
12,000
DARTH MAUL
12,000

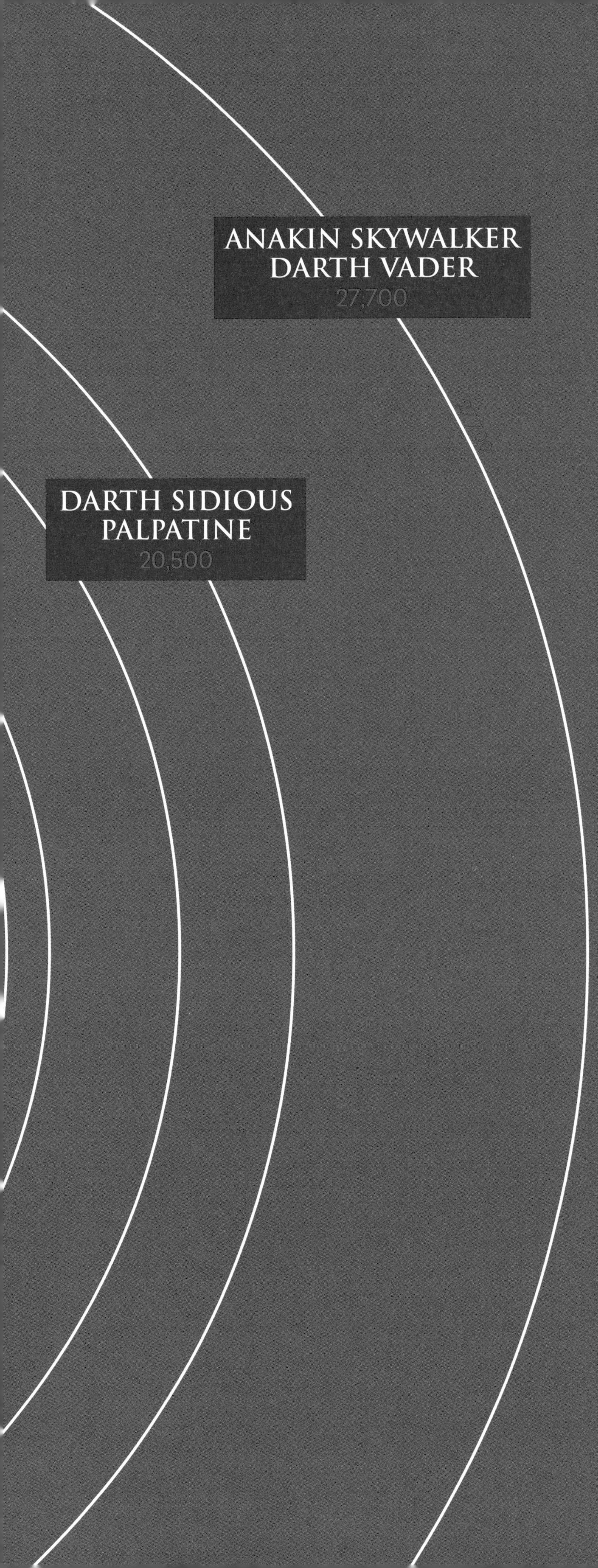

**ANAKIN SKYWALKER
DARTH VADER**
27,700

**DARTH SIDIOUS
PALPATINE**
20,500

*Myth or reality?
The debate still rages
among fans, but one thing
is sure: in the Star Wars
mythology, they're well
and truly present.*

AVERAGE COUNT FOR A
JEDI: 10,000

MINIMUM REQUIRED TO
BECOME A JEDI: 7,000

●

JEDI

●

SITH

●

HUMANS

●

ANIMALS

●

MACHINE

AVERAGE MAN
L = 0.2m
W = 0.6m
H = 1.80m

SLAVE I
L = 21.5m
W= 21.3m
H = 7.8m

Y-WING
L = 16m
W = 7.9m
H = 2.9m

74-Z SPEEDER-BIKE
L = 3m
W = 60cm
H = 60cm

JABBA'S BARGE
L = 30m
W= 9.8m
H = 5.3m

B-WING
L = 16.9m
W = 2.9m
H = 2.5m (7.3m wings extended)

MILLENNIUM FALCON
L = 34.37m
W = 25.61m
H = 8.27m
(9.77m with legs)

AT-AT
L = 20m
W = 5m
H = 22.5m

X-WING
L = 12.5m
W = 11.5m
H = 1.9m (2.6m wings extended)

TIE FIGHTER
L = 8.99m
W = 9m
H = 11m

SANDCRAWLER
L = 36.8m
W = 10m
H = 20m

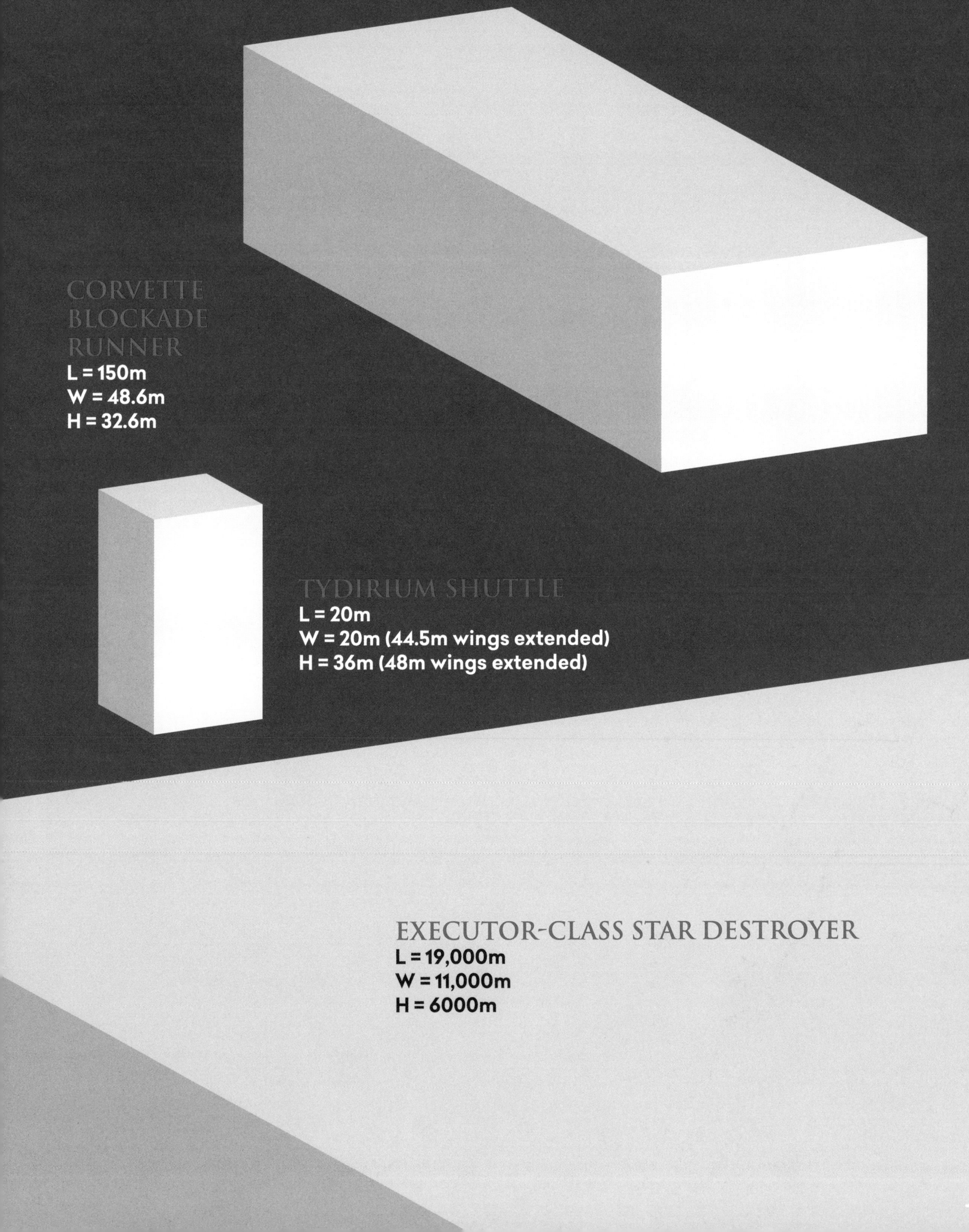

CORVETTE BLOCKADE RUNNER
L = 150m
W = 48.6m
H = 32.6m

TYDIRIUM SHUTTLE
L = 20m
W = 20m (44.5m wings extended)
H = 36m (48m wings extended)

EXECUTOR-CLASS STAR DESTROYER
L = 19,000m
W = 11,000m
H = 6000m

20 YEARS LATER, HISTORY MIRRORS ITSELF,
... BUT NOT COMPLETELY.

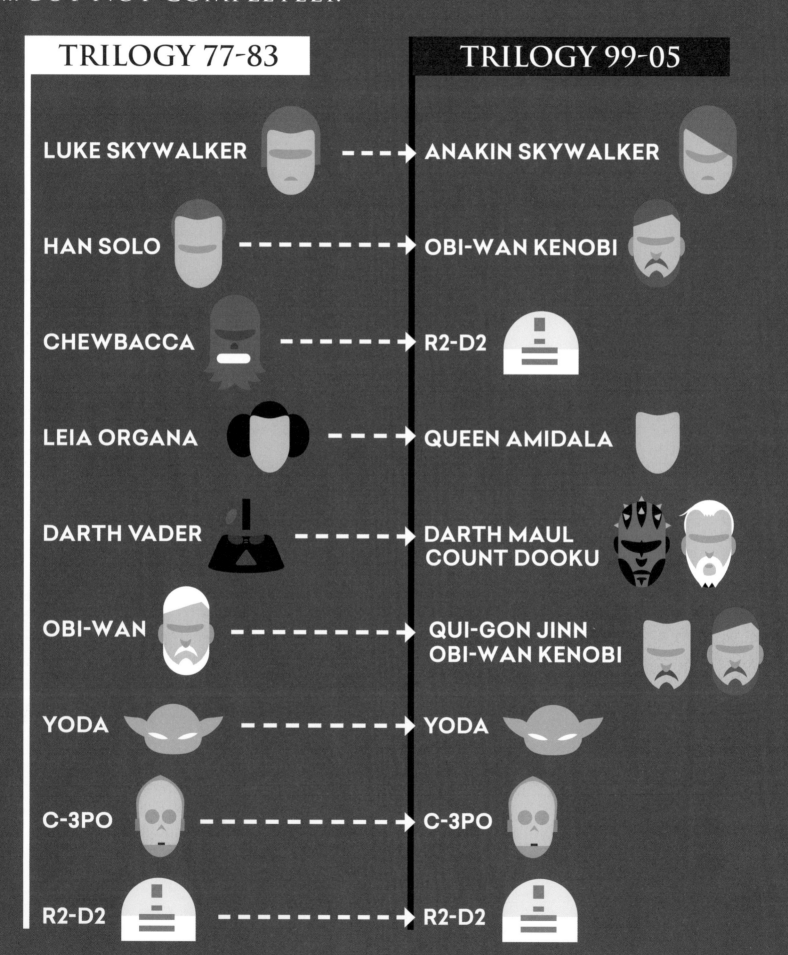

TRILOGY 77-83

TRILOGY 99-05

LUKE SKYWALKER - - - → ANAKIN SKYWALKER

HAN SOLO - - - - → OBI-WAN KENOBI

CHEWBACCA - - - - → R2-D2

LEIA ORGANA - - - → QUEEN AMIDALA

DARTH VADER - - - → DARTH MAUL
COUNT DOOKU

OBI-WAN - - - - → QUI-GON JINN
OBI-WAN KENOBI

YODA - - - - → YODA

C-3PO - - - - → C-3PO

R2-D2 - - - - → R2-D2

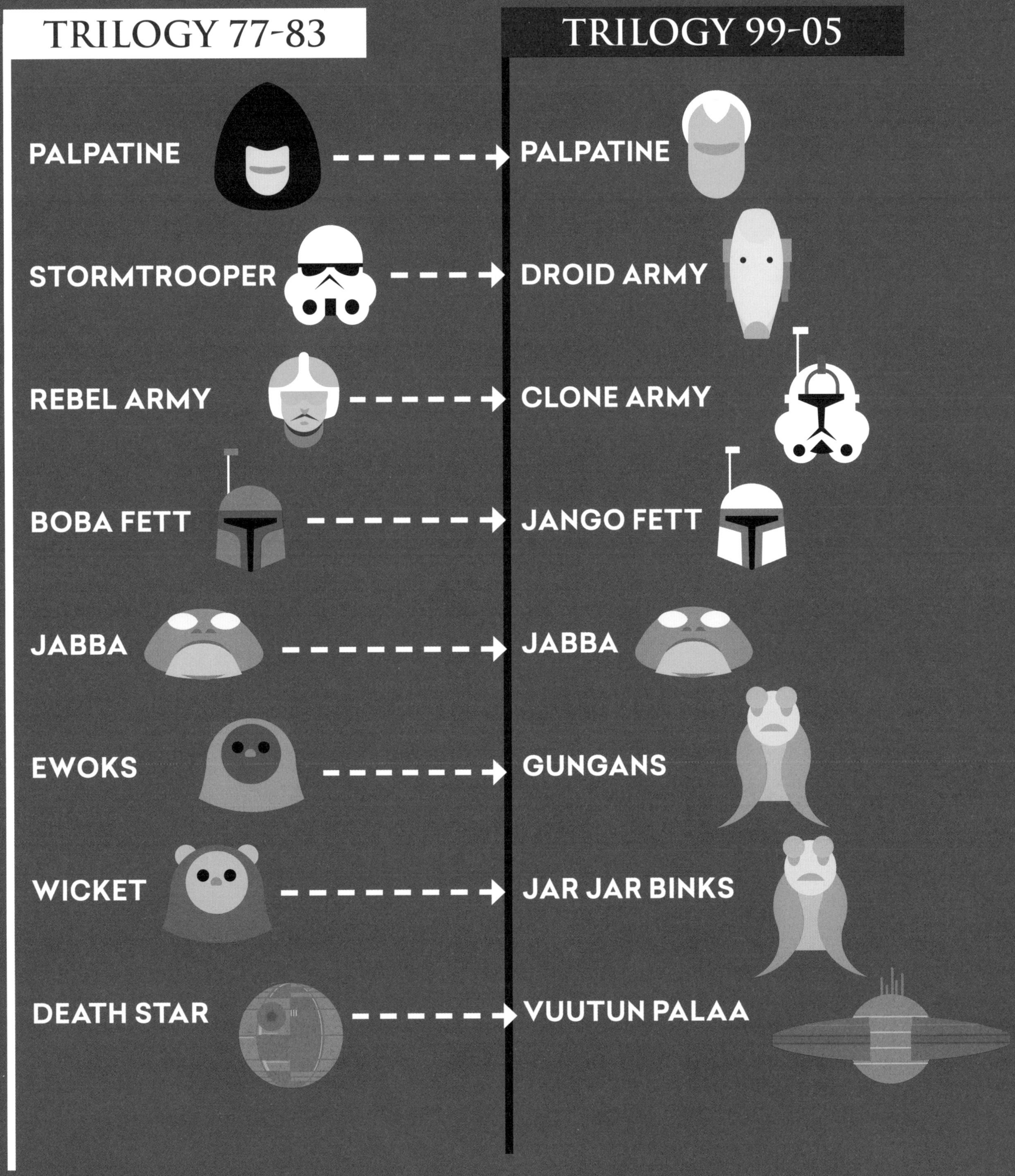

TRILOGY 77-83
TRILOGY 99-05
PALPATINE
PALPATINE
STORMTROOPER
DROID ARMY
REBEL ARMY
CLONE ARMY
BOBA FETT
JANGO FETT
JABBA
JABBA
EWOKS
GUNGANS
WICKET
JAR JAR BINKS
DEATH STAR
VUUTUN PALAA

MUSICAL INTERLUDE

THE *IMPERIAL MARCH* IS A CLASSIC THEME FOREVER ASSOCIATED WITH *STAR WARS* IN THE COLLECTIVE UNCONSCIOUS. IT REMAINS THE CENTRAL PIECE OF JOHN WILLIAMS' SCORE WHICH IS AS CONSISTENT AS IT IS SEMINAL.

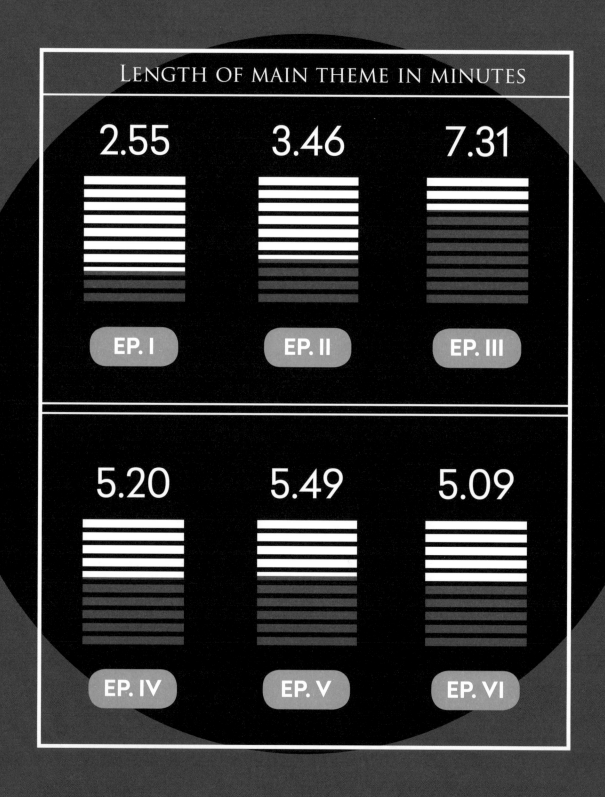

LENGTH OF MAIN THEME IN MINUTES

| 2.55 | 3.46 | 7.31 |
| EP. I | EP. II | EP. III |

| 5.20 | 5.49 | 5.09 |
| EP. IV | EP. V | EP. VI |

THE PHANTOM MENACE

PIECES
17

SIDES
4

EP. I

LENGTH
74.23 min

HIT
*Duel of
the Fates*

ATTACK OF THE CLONES

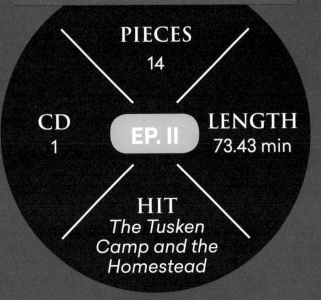

PIECES
14

CD
1

EP. II

LENGTH
73.43 min

HIT
*The Tusken
Camp and the
Homestead*

REVENGE OF THE SITH

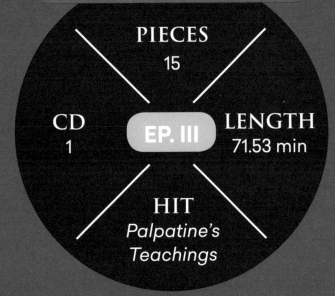

PIECES
15

CD
1

EP. III

LENGTH
71.53 min

HIT
*Palpatine's
Teachings*

A NEW HOPE

PIECES
16

SIDES
4

EP. IV

LENGTH
74.58 min

HIT
Cantina Band

THE EMPIRE STRIKES BACK

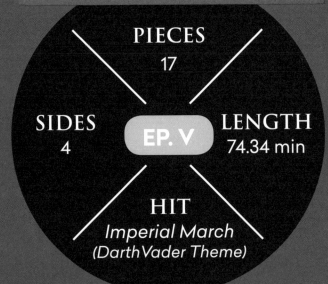

PIECES
17

SIDES
4

EP. V

LENGTH
74.34 min

HIT
*Imperial March
(Darth Vader Theme)*

RETURN OF THE JEDI

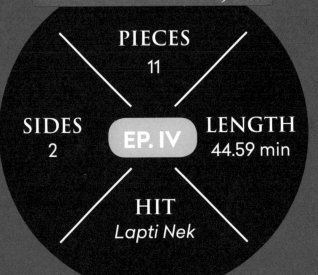

PIECES
11

SIDES
2

EP. IV

LENGTH
44.59 min

HIT
Lapti Nek

FIRSTTRILOGY

[1977-1983]

CHARACTER HEIGHT

OBI-WAN
KENOBI
1.82M

HAN SOLO
1.80M

LUKE
SKYWALKER
1.72M

C-3PO
1.67M

LEIA ORGANA
1.50M

R2-D2
96 CM

YODA
66 CM

RANCOR
5M

DARTH VADER
2.02M

CHEWBACCA
2.28M

THE EMPEROR
1.73M

ABBA THE HUTT
1.73M

LANDO
CALRISSIAN
1.78M

SALACIOUS CRUMB
70CM

JAWA
1M

EWOK
80CM

MILLENNIUM FALCON

DIMENSIONS

Height	Length	Depth
34.37m	25.61m	8.27m

SPEED
1050 Km/h

WEIGHT
100 tons

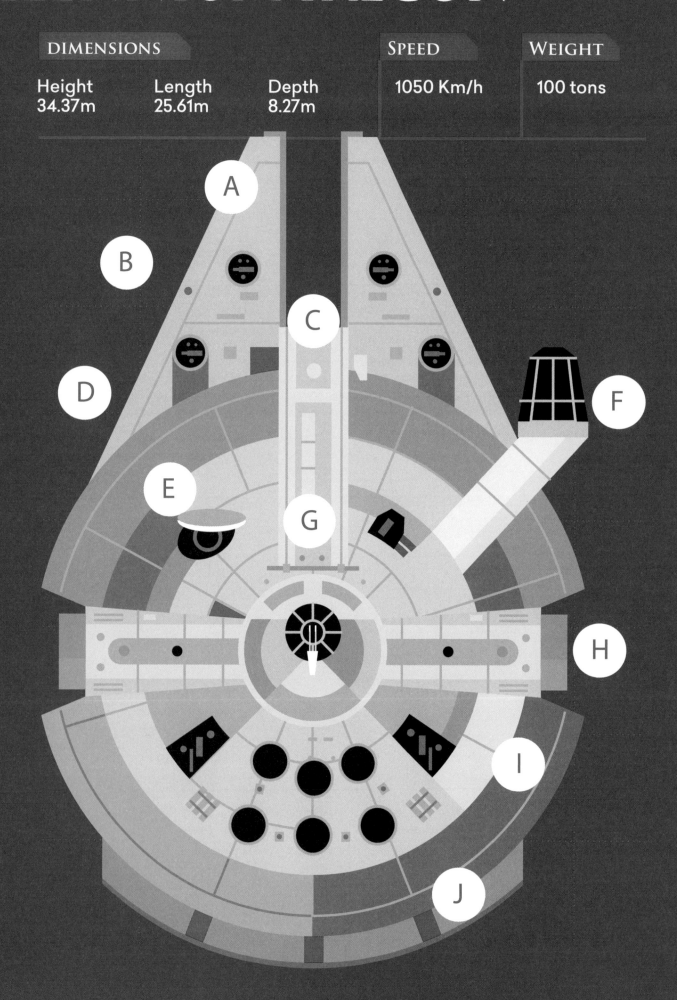

RANGE

1 AN	1 AN	1 AN	1 AN	1 AN	1 AN

ENGINES

2	Girodyne SRB42

HYPERDRIVE

Class 0.5

WEAPONRY

2	Corellian Engineering Corporation AG-2G quad laser cannons
1	AX-108 BlasTech "Ground Buzzer" blaster
2	Arakyd ST2 quad concussion missile launchers
1	Ganathan electric cannon
1	Mark VII tractor beam generator
	Mines
	Anti-missile propulsors

SHIELDS

1	1 Torplex deflector shield generator
1	1 Novaldex shield generator
1	1 Kuat Drive Yards deflector shield generator
1	1 Nordoxicon-38 anti-concussion shield generator
1	1 deflector navigation system

STRUCTURE

A — Forward mooring mandible

B — Equipment access bay

C — Concussion missile launcher

D — Deflector shield generator

E — Tracking radar

F — Cockpit

G — Quadrilaser battery

H — Escape pod

I — Armour plate

J — Ion flux turbine

SMALL CRAFT

1 POD

PASSENGERS

6

CREW REQUIRED

2

STAR DESTROYER

IMPERIAL-I CLASS

DIMENSIONS			SPEED	WEIGHT
Height 1600 m	Length 900 m	Depth 450 m	975 Km/h	36,000 tons

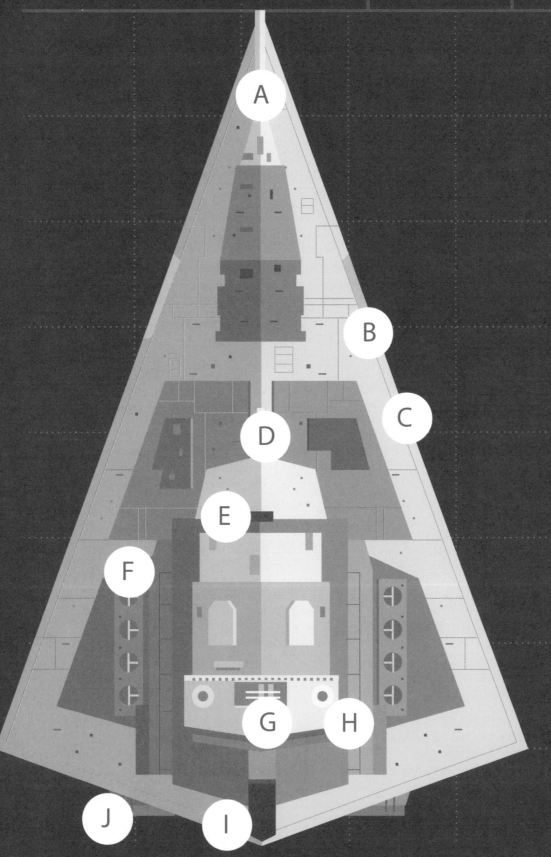

RANGE

1 AN   1 AN   1 AN   1 AN   1 AN   1 AN

ENGINES

3 DKY Destroyer-I ion engines

4 Cygnus Spaceworks Gemon-4

WEAPONRY

8 Octuple turbolasers or ion cannons

50 heavy turbolaser batteries

60 turbolaser batteries

26 supplementary turbolaser batteries (optional)

20 heavy ion cannons

10 Phylon Q7 tractor beam projectors

STRUCTURE

A — Computer-targeted turbolaser

B — Computer-targeted ion cannons

C — Computer-targeted turbolaser

D — Control room

E — Ion cannons

F — Turbolaser towers

G — Communication tower

H — Deflector shield generator dome

I — Solar ionisation reactor

J — Cygnus Spaceworks Germon 4

HYPERDRIVE

Class 2

SHIELDS

2 KDY ISD-72x deflector shield generator domes

SMALL CRAFT

72 TIE fighters

8 Lambda-class shuttles

8 Delta-class troop transports

5 assault shuttles

1 Gamma-class shuttle

20 AT-AT

30 AT-ST

Other vehicles

PASSENGERS

5000

CREW REQUIRED

9700

IN A GALAXY FAR, FAR AWAY

DEATH STAR SUPER LASER
20 BILLION CREDITS

T-14 SUPERSPEED GENERATOR
20,000 CREDITS

LIGHTSABER
3000 CREDITS

STORMTROOPER'S BLASTER
1000 CREDITS

CHEWBACCA'S BOWCASTER
FREE

SECRET TRIP BETWEEN TATOOINE AND ALDERAAN
17,000 CREDITS

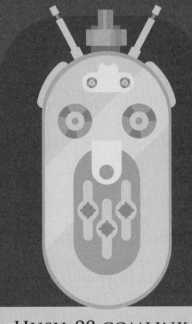

HUSH-98 COMLINK

4000 CREDITS

GREEDO'S LIFE

4100 CREDITS

A DEATH STAR

1 TRILLION CREDITS

BLASTECH DL-44 (HAN SOLO'S BLASTER)

750 CREDITS

BRINGING SOMEONE BACK FOR A BOUNTY WITHOUT A WORK PERMIT

245 CREDITS

BOBA FETT'S DAILY EXPENSES

500 CREDITS

HIRE THE CANTINA BAND FOR A WEDDING (FIGRIN D'AN & THE MODAL NODES)

3000 CREDITS

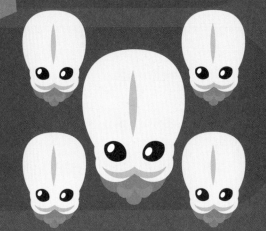

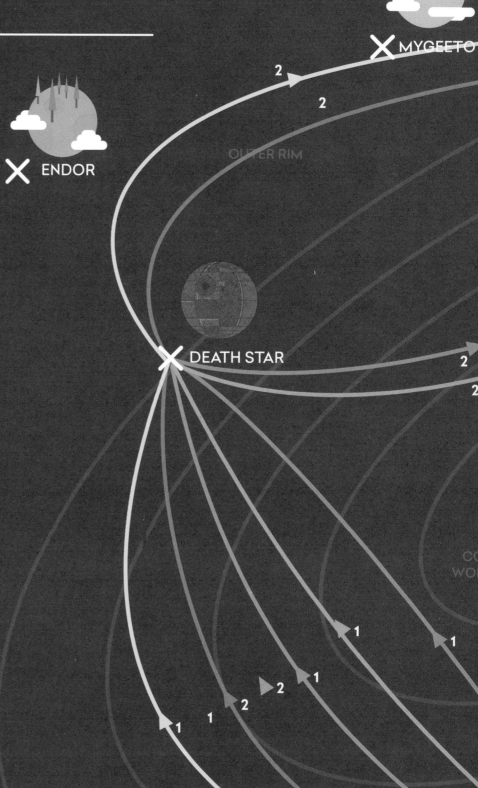

✕ MYGEETO

2

2

OUTER RIM

✕ ENDOR

✕ HOTH

✕ BESPIN

DEATH STAR ✕

2

2

✕ MUSTAFAR

1

1

1

2

2

1

2

1

✕ NABOO

✕ DAGOBAH

✕ UTAPAU

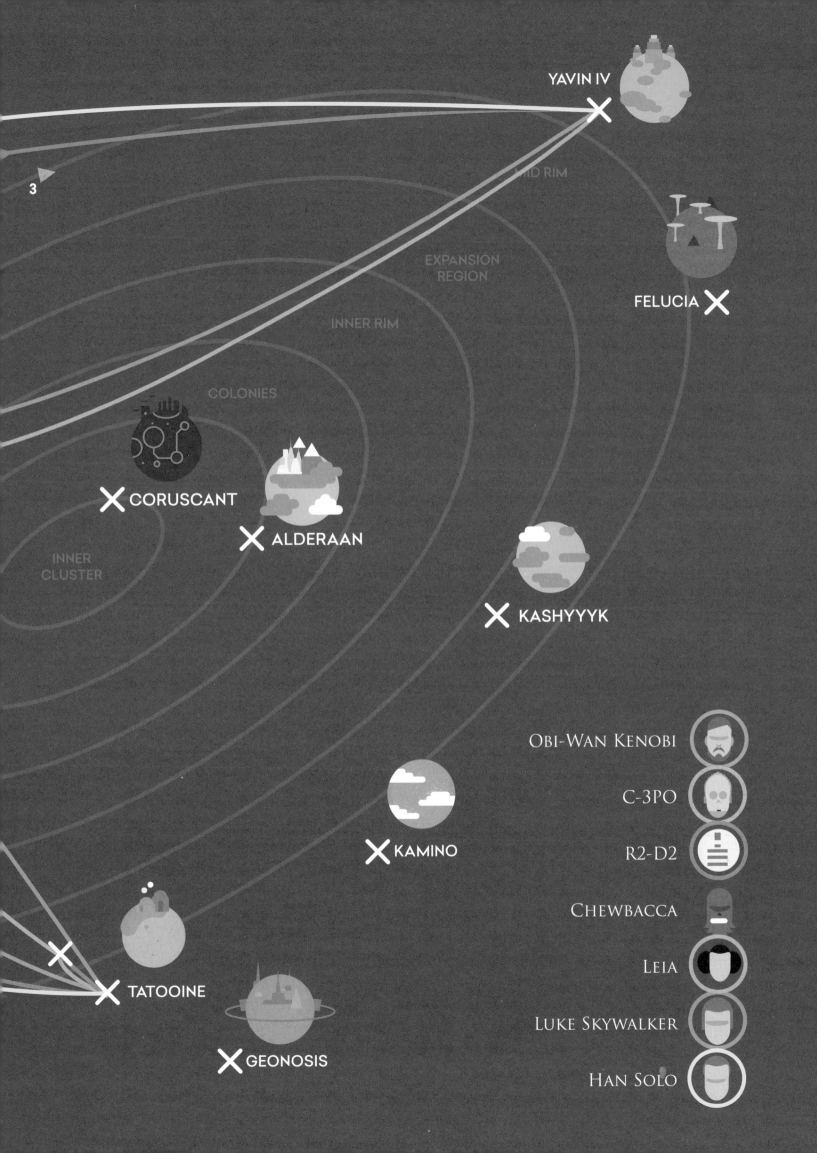

YAVIN IV

MID RIM

EXPANSION
REGION

INNER RIM

FELUCIA

COLONIES

CORUSCANT

ALDERAAN

KASHYYYK

INNER
CLUSTER

OBI-WAN KENOBI

C-3PO

KAMINO

R2-D2

CHEWBACCA

LEIA

TATOOINE

LUKE SKYWALKER

GEONOSIS

HAN SOLO

FINAL BATTLE

LOCATION : Space - Death Star

LENGTH/BEGINNING: 1:45:01 **END :** 1:57:16 = 12.15 minutes

WHAT'S AT STAKE: destruction of the Death Star

BEGINNING: lift-off of the rebel fleet on Yavin 4
END: Darth Vader escapes

FORCES PRESENT: 33 Rebel Alliance ships vs the Empire

KEY SHIPS

22 X-WINGS

8 Y-WINGS

2 R-22 SPEARHEAD

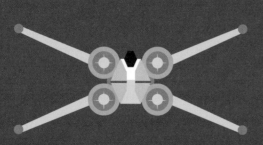

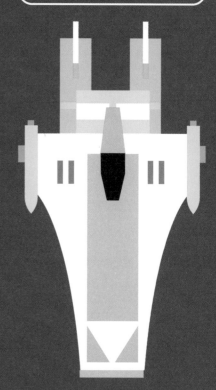

1 MILLENNIUM FALCON

VS

THE DEATH STAR

2 TIE FIGHTERS

1 ADVANCED TIE

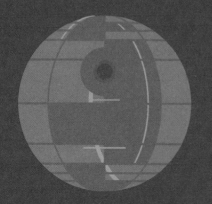

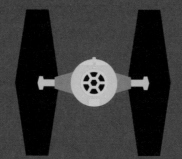

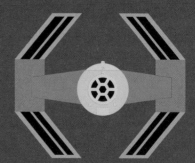

COMMANDERS

REBELS

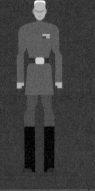

GENERAL BOB HUDSOL	GENERAL JAN DODONNA	PRINCESS LEIA ORGANA

EMPIRE

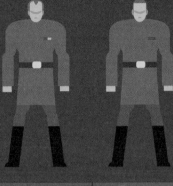

DARTH VADER	GRAND MOFF WILHUFF TARKIN	ADMIRAL CONAN ANTONIO MOTTI	GRAND GENERAL CASSIO TAGGE

KEY CHARACTERS

REBELS

HAN SOLO

EMPIRE

DARTH VADER

REBELS

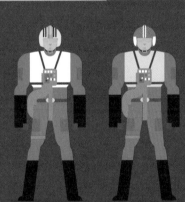
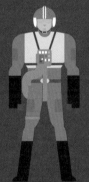
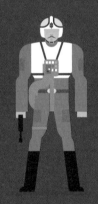
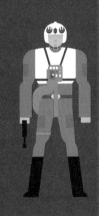

GARVEN DREIS (RED LEADER)	WEDGE ANTILLES (RED 2)	BIGGS DARKLIGHTER (RED 3)	TIREE (GOLD 2)

REBELS

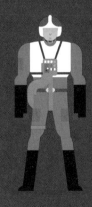

JEK TONO PORKINS (RED 6)	THERON NETT (RED 10)	PUCK NAECO (RED 12)	JON VANDER (GOLD LEADER)	LUKE SKYWALKER (RED 5)	KEYAN FARLANDER (GOLD 7)

CHRONOLOGY AND EVENTS

Beginning: lift-off of the rebel fleet on Yavin 4

First strike: Biggs Darklighter
vs
turbolaser battery at 1.47.18

First shot: an ion cannon fired from the Death Star at 1.46.00

1st rebel loss: Red 6 at 1.47.29 (hit by the turbolaser battery explosion)

1st Empire loss: a stormtrooper on the Death Star (explosion of the turbolaser battery) at 1.47.19

BOOM!

1st appearance of the Force: Obi-Wan speaks to Luke at 1.47.40

TIE fighters appear at 1.48.00

1st X-wing destroyed by a TIE fighter at 1.48.11

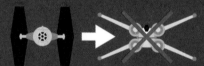

1st TIE fighter destroyed: Luke at 1.48.31

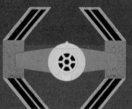

1st feat of Wedge Antilles: destroys a TIE fighter at 1.49.21

Luke is hit at 1.48.5

1st incursion into the trench: Gold Leader at 1.49.45

TIE fighter destroys 1 X-wing (Red 12) at 1.52.41

Luke, Biggs and Wedge enter the trench at 1.53.50

Red Leader misses the target at 1.52.49

Wedge is hit at 1.54.36 and aborts

Obi-Wan speaks at 1.55.38

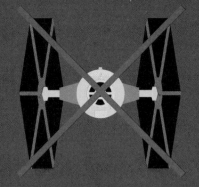

TURNING POINT
Millennium Falcon arrives, destroys a TIE fighter at **1.56.47**

Torpedoes launched by Luke at **1.57.04**

2 X-wings (Luke & Wedge),
1 Y-wing (Keyan Farlander),
and the *Millennium Falcon* escape.

BOOM!

BOOM!

The Death Star explodes at **1.57.16**

BOOM!

Darth Vader escapes

IN BRIEF

DARTH VADER'S SCORE

3 Y-WINGS
at **1.50.40** (Gold 2)
at **1.50.55** (Gold Leader)
at **1.51.03** (Gold 5)

2 X-WINGS
(Red 10) at **1.52.31**
(Red Leader) at **1.53.19**

Biggs Darklighter at **1.55.07**
R2-D2 at **1.56.14**

DEATH STAR

DIMENSION	SPEED	STRUCTURE	
120km diameter	10 MGLT	**3**	docking bays

LIFESPAN
29 BBY–0 ABY

COST
1,000,000,000 credits

CAPACITY
1 million kilotons

12 Zones

A — superlaser focusing lens ("eye")
B — Equatorial trench
C — Polar trench
D — Meridian trench (north/south)
E — "Urban" surface blocks
F — Quadanium external hull

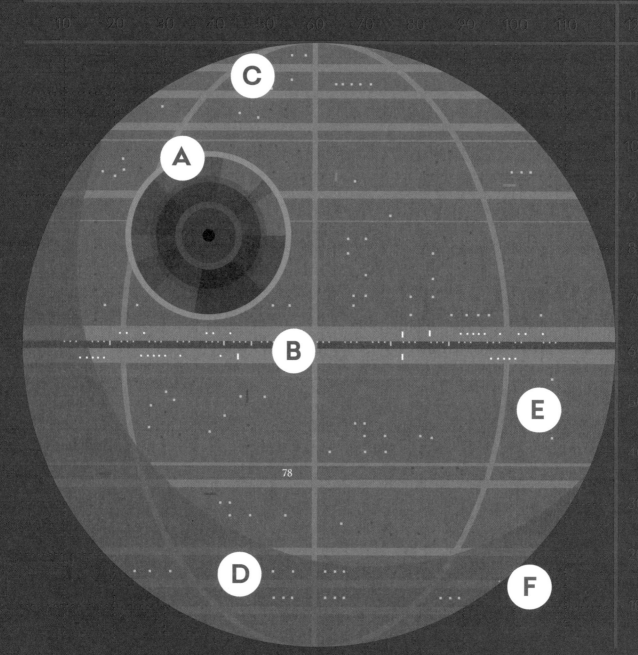

RANGE

| 1 AN | 1 AN | 1 AN | 1 AN | 1 AN | 1 AN |

MOTOR

| 1 | motor |

HYPERDRIVE

4.0 / 123 generators

WEAPONRY

1	Superlaser (range 47,060,000 km)
5,000	Taim & Bak D6 turbolaser batteries
5,000	Taim & Bak XX9 heavy turbolasers
2,500	SFS L-s 4.9 laser cannons
2,500	Borstel MS-1 ion cannons
/	SB-920 laser cannons
768	Phylon tractor beam generators
/	Particle blasters
/	Magnetic machine guns
/	Proton torpedoes
/	Canons

SHIELDS

| 2 | KDY ISD-72x deflector shield generator domes |

SMALL CRAFT

7000	TIE fighters
4	assault cruisers
3600	assault shuttles
1400	AT-AT
1400	AT-ST
1860	troop transports

CREW

342,953	regular crew		
27,048	officers		
607,360	troops including	25,984	stormtroopers
		57,278	gunners
167,216	pilots		
285,675	maintenance		
42,782	support staff		
843,342	passengers		
400,000	droids		

CHALMUN'S CANTINA

ADDRESS:
3112 OUTER KERNER WAY,
MOS EISLEY, TATOOINE

17		TABLES
1		BAR
58		SEATS
102		MAX CAPACITY (HUMANS) AT THE MOMENT OF GREEDO'S MURDER
37		ALIENS
7		HUMANS
2		DROIDS

A — Cellar staircase

B — Office

C — Drink dispenser

D — Bar

E — Kiosk

F — Alcove table

G — Droid detector

H — Entry vestibule

I — Counter

J — Main door

K — Rear door

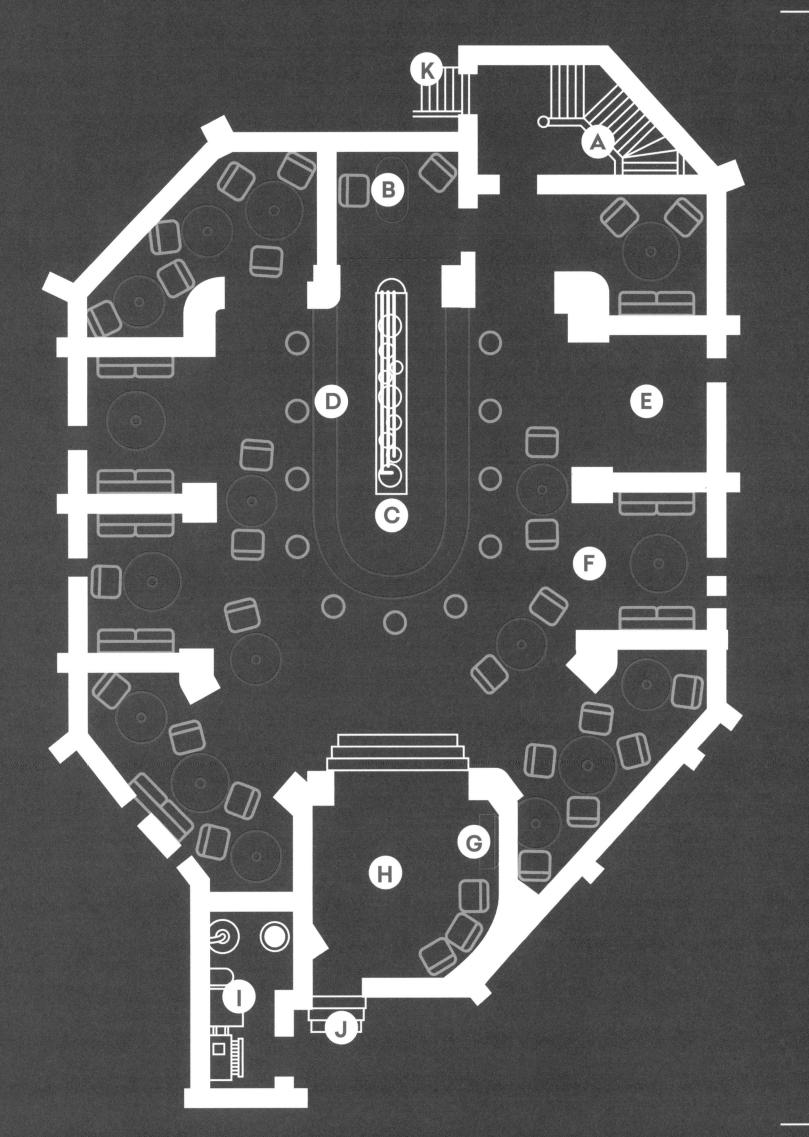

Episode V – The Empire Strikes Back
Character Journeys

MYGEETO

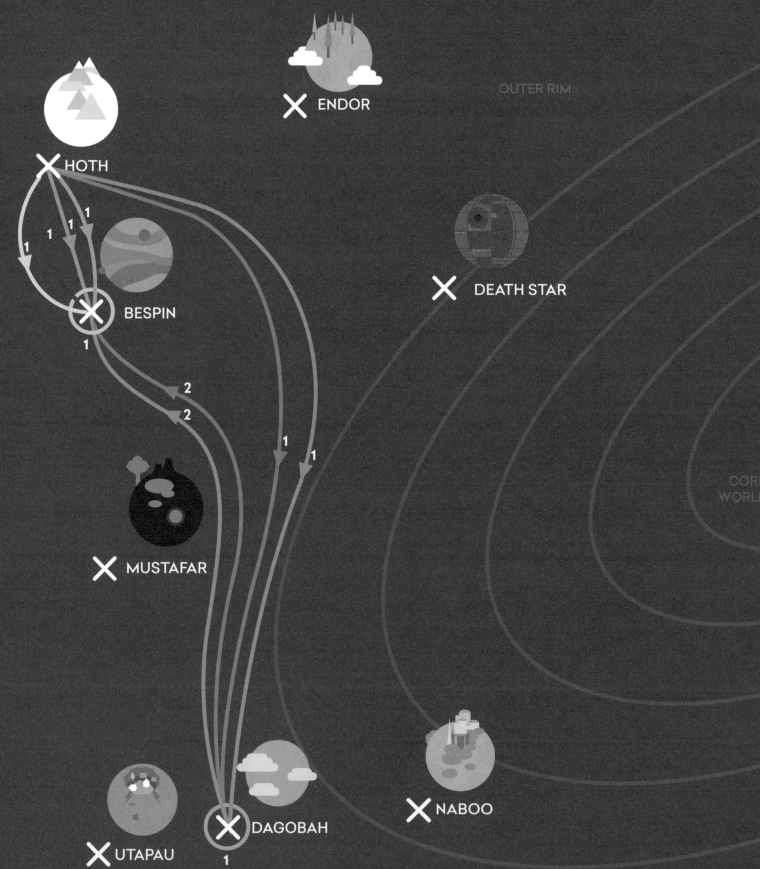

ENDOR

HOTH

DEATH STAR

BESPIN

MUSTAFAR

UTAPAU

DAGOBAH

NABOO

OUTER RIM

CORE WORLD

 YAVIN 4 X

 FELUCIA X

MID RIM

EXPANSION REGION

INNER CLUSTER

COLONIES

 X

 CORUSCANT

1

X ALDERAAN

INNER CLUSTER

X KASHYYYK

 C-3PO

 R2-D2

 YODA

 PALPATINE

 CHEWBACCA

 BOBA FETT

 PRINCESS LEIA

 LUKE SKYWALKER

HAN SOLO

X KAMINO

X TATOOINE

 X GEONOSIS

FINAL BATTLE

LOCATION : Cloud City - cryogenic chamber/landing bay

LENGTH/BEGINNING: 1.40.25 END : 1.52.13 = 11.48 minutes

WHAT'S AT STAKE: Luke vs Vader / Lando must escape from Cloud City

BEGINNING: a door closes on R2-D2

END: the *Millennium Falcon* launches

FORCES PRESENT: Jedi vs Sith/Lando Calrissian vs the Empire

KEY CHARACTERS

EMPIRE

REBELS

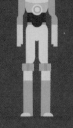

| DARTH VADER | LUKE SKYWALKER | PRINCESS LEIA ORGANA | LANDO CALRISSIAN | R2-D2 | C-3PO | CHEWBACCA |

1) CHRONOLOGY AND EVENTS:
ON LEVEL 3

Vader's arrival at 1.40.48

Luke ignites his lightsaber at 1.41.06

Vader ignites his at 1.41.09

Vader disarms Luke at 1.43.59

First clash at 1.41.17

Luke escapes from the cryogenic chamber at 1.44.27

Luke falls into the cryogenic chamber at 1.44.22

Luke pushes Vader into the void at 1.45.13

"Impressive. Most impressive."
Darth Vader at 1.44.37

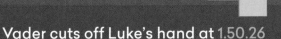

Luke goes through the window at 1.46.42

Move to lower level at 1.45.38

Move to the catwalk at 1.47.00

Vader cuts off Luke's hand at 1.50.26

Luke wounds Vader at 1.50.21

"I am your father." Darth Vader at 1.51.17

"Join me, and together we can rule the galaxy as father and son."
Darth Vader at 1.51.52

Luke throws himself into the void at 1.52.133

2) CHRONOLOGY AND EVENTS:
ON LEVEL 1

Cloud City Guards surround the stormtroopers at 1.41.50

Chewie strangles Lando at 1.42.15

Boba Fett loads Han Solo in his carbonite at 1.42.55

R2-D2 joins the group at 1.43.08

Boba Fett escapes at 1.43.37

Lando evacuates Cloud City at 1.47.25

R2-D2 clears the security system at 1.48.22

The *Millennium Falcon* lifts at 1.49.21

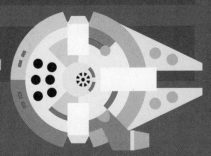

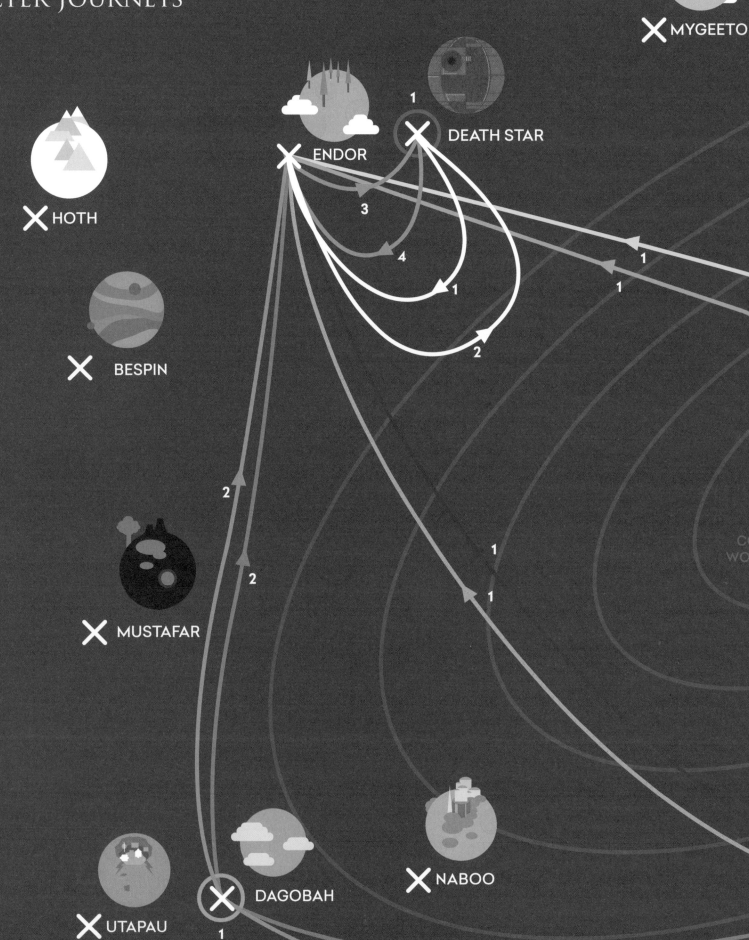

MYGEETO

DEATH STAR

ENDOR

1

3

4

1

2

HOTH

BESPIN

1

1

2

2

1

1

MUSTAFAR

NABOO

DAGOBAH

UTAPAU

1

1

1

OUTER
BORDER

YAVIN 4 ✕

MID RIM

EXPANSION
REGION

FELUCIA ✕

INNER RIM

COLONIES

✕ CORUSCANT

✕ ALDERAAN

INNER
CLUSTER

✕ KASHYYYK

C-3PO

R2-D2

Yoda

Palpatine

✕ KAMINO

Chewbacca

Boba Fett

Princess Leia

✕ TATOOINE

Luke Skywalker

1

✕ GEONOSIS

Darth Vader

Han Solo

FINAL BATTLE

LOCATIONS: Endor / Death Star / Space

LENGTH /BEGINNING: 1.28.51 **END :** 2.03.21 = 34.30 minutes

WHAT'S AT STAKE: deactivate the Death Star's shield, overthrow Palpatine and destroy the Death Star

FORCES PRESENT: Rebels & Ewoks vs Empire/Jedi vs Sith/Rebels vs Death Star

KEY CHARACTERS

REBELS

CHEWBACCA	HAN SOLO	PRINCESS LEIA ORGANA	R2-D2	C-3PO	PAPLOO	WICKET

REBELS

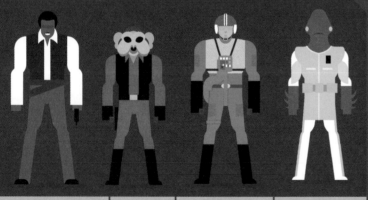

LANDO CALRISSIAN	NIEN NUNB	WEDGE ANTILLES	ADMIRAL ACKBAR

JEDI

LUKE SKYWALKER

EMPIRE

DARTH VADER	PALPATINE

KEY VEHICLES

HOME ONE

Y-WING

X-WING

TIE FIGHTER

MILLENNIUM FALCON

A-WING

B-WING

SPEEDER BIKES

TIE INTERCEPTOR

+ REBEL FRIGATES

AT-ST

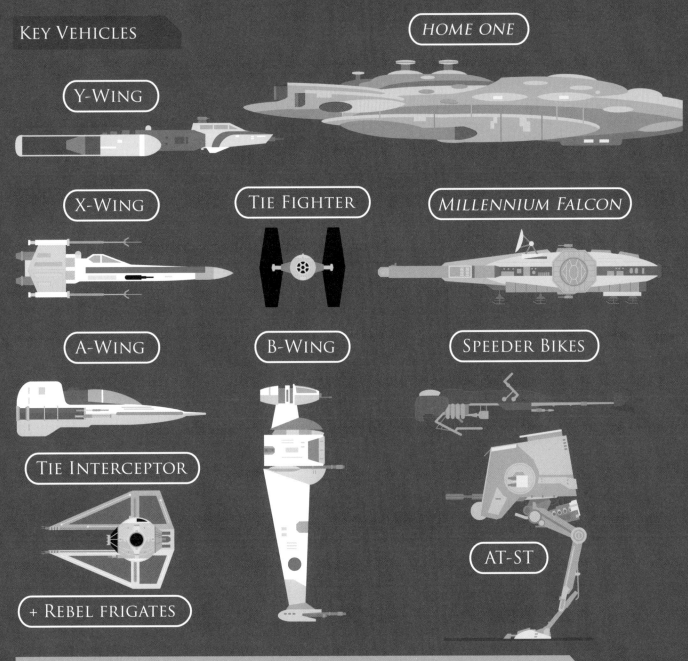

1) CHRONOLOGY AND EVENTS:
BUNKER / ENDOR

4 scout troopers protect the bunker

Paploo steals the speeder bike at 1.28.51
pursued by 3 scout troopers

Paploo jumps off the speeder bike at 1.29.35

Last trooper arrested by the rebels at 1.29.44

Bunker opens at 1.29.48

Arrival in the control room at 1.33.20

Empire reaches the bunker at 1.33.40

Han, Leia, Chewie arrested. "You rebel scum" at 1.33.57

C-3PO distracts the Imperial troops at 1.37.11

Han and Leia freed at 1.38.26

R2-D2 and C-3PO join Han and Leia at 1.42.47

2 Ewoks explode at 1.43.32. One dies.

BOOM!

First AT-ST destroyed by Chewbacca at 1.46.30

Another at 1.47.19   BOOM!

Another at 1.47.46   BOOM!

Bunker sabotaged at 1.51.35

First Ewok attack on stormtroopers at 1.37.35

Wicket knocks himself out at 1.39.32

R2-D2 draws fire at 1.43.00

Chewbacca takes over an AT-ST at 1.46.19 / **TURNING POINT**

First vehicle destroyed by an Ewok: a speeder bike at 1.47.15

An AT-ST at 1.47.33   BOOM!

Leia is wounded at 1.47.55

Bunker explodes at 1.54.41

BOOM!

2) CHRONOLOGY AND EVENTS:
DEATH STAR

Luke surrenders to Darth Vader at 1.23.14

Darth Vader to Luke at 1.25.25
"It is too late for me, my son."

Vader's *Tydirium* lifts at 1.26.19

Luke meets the Emperor at 1.30.46

The Emperor tells Luke that he knows the rebels' plans at 1.32.10

Luke witnesses the attack at 1.35.36

Death Star fires for the first time at 1.41.55

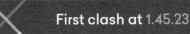

Luke retrieves his lightsaber at 1.45.22

Vader ignites his lightsaber at 1.45.22

First clash at 1.45.23

Luke makes Vader fall at 1.48.50

Luke stops fighting at 1.49.05

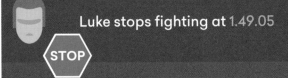

Vader resumes the duel at 1.49.34

Vader officially wavers. "Your thoughts betray you, father." – Luke Skywalker to Darth Vader at 1.50.00. Interruption of duel.

Vader discovers Leia's existence at 1.52.21
TURNING POINT

Luke resumes the duel at 1.52.48

Luke strikes Vader down at 1.53.21

Luke cuts off Vader's hand at 1.53.24

Luke turns away from the dark side at 1.54.09 "Never. I'll never turn to the dark side." – Luke to the Emperor

The Emperor attacks Luke at 1.55.14

<u>RETURN OF THE JEDI</u>
Vader seizes the Emperor at 1.56.55

Destruction of the Emperor at 1.57.10

IN BRIEF

NUMBER OF LIGHTSABER CLASHES:
49 (green vs red)

3) CHRONOLOGY AND EVENTS:
SPACE / DEATH STAR

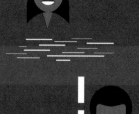

Lando engages
lightspeed at 1.27.43

Millennium Falcon arrives
within range of Death Star
at 1.34.05

Lando sees the
trap at 1.34.46

"It's a trap!"
Admiral Ackbar at 1.35.09

Appearance of the Imperial Fleet at 1.35.11

First Imperial attack at 1.35.14

Death Star fires for the first time at 1.41.55

Rebel frigate destroyed at 1.41.58

Rebel frigate destroyed at 1.43.58
(by the Death Star's second shot)

Death Star's shield falls at 1.54.53
__TURNING POINT__

The *Millennium Falcon* enters the
Death Star at 1.57.55

The *Millennium Falcon*
loses its deflector shield at 1.58.39

Star Destroyer destroyed at 1.58.52

BOOM!

Super Star Destroyer destroyed at 1.59.30

Wedge hits the bullseye at 2.02.15

BOOM!

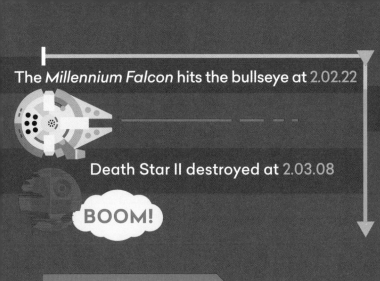

The *Millennium Falcon* hits the bullseye at 2.02.22

The *Millennium Falcon* gets away at 2.03.01

Death Star II destroyed at 2.03.08

BOOM!

TIE DESTROYED

5 FIGHTERS
7 INTERCEPTORS
3 BY THE *MILLENNIUM FALCON*
TOTAL = 12

WINGS DESTROYED

2 A-WING
3 X-WING
1 Y-WING
TOTAL = 6

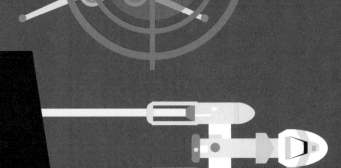

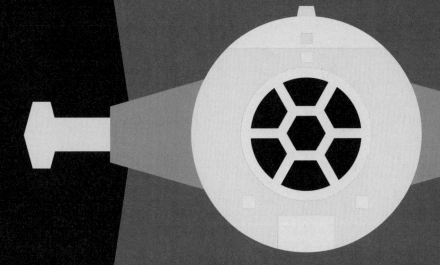

DIMENSION	SPEED
160 km/diameter	20 MGLT

LIFE SPAN

29 BBY–0 ABY

COST

1,000,000,000 credits

CAPACITY

1 million kilotons

STRUCTURE

1   Docking bay

12   Zones

A — Superlaser focusing lens ("eye")

B — Equatorial trench

C — North command sector

D — South command sector

E — Reactor core (internal)

F — Exposed superstructure

10   20   30   40   50   60   70   80   90   100   110   160 KM

110
100
90
80
70
60
50
40
30
20
10

C
A
B
E
D
F

RANGE

1 AN	1 AN	1 AN	1 AN	1 AN	1 AN

MOTOR

/	incomplete

HYPERDRIVE

3.0

WEAPONRY

1	Superlaser (range 47,060,000 km)
15,000	Taim & Bak D6 turbolaser batteries
15,000	Taim & Bak XX9 heavy turbolasers
7,500	SFS L-s 4.9 laser cannons
5,000	Borstel MS-1 ion cannons
768	Phylon tractor beam generators

SMALL CRAFT

7200	TIE fighters
16	Destroyers
3600	*Tydirium* shuttles
2480	Skipray patrol boats
1400	AT-AT
1400	AT-ST
1420	Repulsor tanks
1420	Repulsor craft
4843	HAVw A5 Juggernauts
178	PX-4 mobile bases
355	HAVr A9 flying fortresses
1860	Troop transports

CREW

485,560	Regular crew		
27,048	Officers		
1,295,950	Troops including	127,570	stormtroopers
		152,275	gunners
334,432	Pilots		
75,860	Maintenance		

TOTAL : 224,190 CREDITS

1 DUMPED CARGO :	**12,400 credits**
1 DEAD EMPLOYEE (GREEDO): :	**4100 credits**
ADVANCES ON THE *MILLENNIUM FALCON*:	**125,640 credits**
BOUNTY NOTICES:	**320 credits**
BOBA FETT BOUNTY:	**5000 credits** (500 /day)
EXTRA BOUNTIES:	**2000 credits** (50 credits /day/hunter)
INTEREST, 50%:	**74,730 credits**

WHAT DOES A JEDI USE EACH ITEM FOR?

A GLOWROD

[flashlight]

A TOOLBOX

[for lightsaber repair]

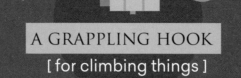

A GRAPPLING HOOK

[for climbing things]

A TRANSCEIVER BEACON

[for communicating]

A HUSH-98 COMLINK

[for communicating]

AN A99 AQUATA BREATHER

[for breathing underwater]

A HOLOPROJECTOR

[for communicating]

A LIGHTSABER

[for fighting]

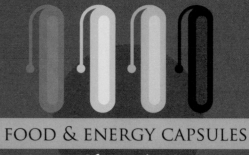

FOOD & ENERGY CAPSULES

[for eating]

CHARACTER COSTUMES THROUGH THE FILMS

DARTH VADER [total : 1]

Ep. IV : 1
Ep. V : 1
Ep. VI : 1

OBI-WAN KENOBI [total : 1]

Ep. IV : 1
Ep. V : 1

CHEWBACCA TOTAL [total : 1]

Ep. IV : 1
Ep. V : 1
Ep. VI : 1

LUKE SKYWALKER [total : 12]

Ep. IV : 4 (Tatooine, stormtrooper, pilot, ceremony)
Ep. V : 5 (Hoth, pilot, Dagobah, Bespin, sickbay)
Ep. VI : 3 (Jedi, pilot, Endor)

HAN SOLO [total : 10]

Ep. IV : 3 (classic, stormtrooper, ceremony)
Ep. V : 3 (Hoth, Bespin, carbonite)
Ep. VI : 4 (carbonite, Jabba, Endor, final)

LEIA [total : 11]

Ep. IV : 3 (classic, Yavin 4, ceremony)
Ep. V : 3 (Hoth, Bespin, sickbay)
Ep. VI : 5 (Boushh, slave, Endor, Ewok, final)

LANDO [total : 3]

Ep. V : 1 (Bespin)
Ep. VI : 2 (Jabba, classic)

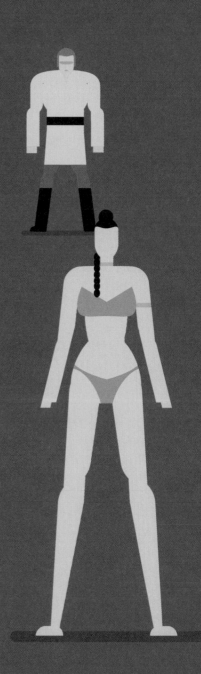

SECONDTRILOGY

[1999-2005]

CHARACTER HEIGHT

QUI-G
1.9

MACE WINDU
1.88M

PADMÉ
AMIDALA
1.65M

DARTH MAUL
1.75M

OBI-WAN
KENOBI
1.79M

ANAKIN
SKYWALKER
1.85M

YODA
66CM

GRIEVOUS
2.3M

JAR JAR BINKS
1.96M

NN

CLONE TROOPER
1.83M

JANGO FETT
1.83M

WATTO
1.37M

SEBULBA
1.12M

✕ MYGEETO

✕ ENDOR

OUTER RIM

✕ HOTH

✕ BESPIN

1

2

▶ 3

2

✕ MUSTAFAR

CO
WORL

3

1

✕ UTAPAU

✕ DAGOBAH

✕ NABOO

1 ▶

YAVIN 4 ✕

EXPANSION
REGION

INNER RIM

FELUCIA ✕

COLONIES

CORUSCANT

✕ALDERAAN

✕ KASHYYYK

INNER
CLUSTER

1

1

✕ KAMINO

2

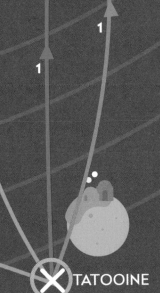
✕TATOOINE

1

✕GEONOSIS

ANAKIN SKYWALKER

PADMÉ AMIDALA

OBI-WAN KENOBI

C-3PO

R2-D2

YODA

PALPATINE

BOONTA RACE IN 32 BBY RACE RESULTS

ANAKIN SKYWALKER

AVERAGE SPEED
655 km/H

TOP SPEED
858 km/H

1

FINISHED 15:42

GASGANO

AVERAGE SPEED
557 km/H

TOP SPEED
850 km/H

2

FINISHED 15:48

ALDAR BEEDO

AVERAGE SPEED
108 km/H

TOP SPEED
845 km/H

3

FINISHED 15:52

ACCIDENTS/ELIMINATION

NEVA KEE, RATTS TYERELL, SEBULBA, ARK ROOSE, WAN SANDAGE, MARS GUO, MAWHONIC, DUD BOLT, CLEGG HOLDFAST, ODY MANDRELL, TEEMTO PAGALIES, BEN QUADINAROS

EBE ENDOCOTT

4

AVERAGE SPEED
827 km/H

TOP SPEED
994 km/H

FINISHED 16:04

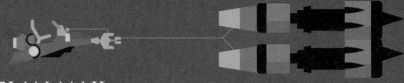

ELAN MAK

5

AVERAGE SPEED
737 km/H

TOP SPEED
819 km/H

FINISHED 16:10

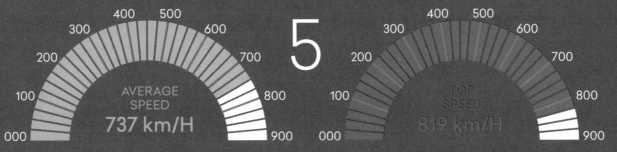

BOLES ROOR

6

AVERAGE SPEED
473 km/H

TOP SPEED
781 km/H

FINISHED 16:42

EPISODE I - THE PHANTOM MENACE
PODRACERS

MARS GUO
Yellow, green, silver
7.24m/790 km/h
2 Plug-2 Behemoth

ALDAR BEEDO
Light blue, yellow
10.59m/823 km/h
2 turbo jets
Mark IV Flat-Twin

DUD BOLT
Metal, orange
7.92m/760 km/h
2 engines

NEVA KEE
Sky blue, white
7.16m/785 km/h
2 engines

GASGANO
Yellow
6.71m/823 km/h
2 engines

RATTS TYERELL

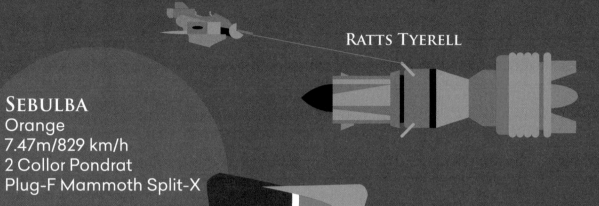

SEBULBA
Orange
7.47m/829 km/h
2 Collor Pondrat
Plug-F Mammoth Split-X

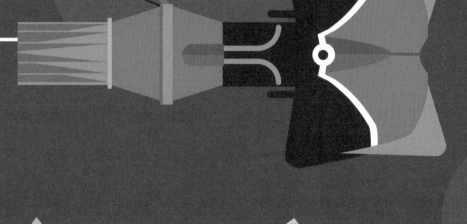

MAWHONIC
Lemon yellow
3.81m/775 km/h
2 engines

WAN SANDAGE
Beige
5.03m/785 km/h

CLEGG HOLDFAST
Metal, red
10.36m/800 km/h
2 engines

Teemto Pagalies
Metal, green, orange
10.67m/775 km/h
2 Long Tail IPG-X1131

Ark "bumpy" roose

Ody Mandrell
Metal, red
8.69m/790 km/h
2 XL 5115

Elan Mak
Light gray,
orange, cream
3.81m/420 km/h
2 KRT 410C

BEN QUADRINOS
Red, metal
4.5m/940 km/h
4 engines

ANAKIN SKYWALKER
Yellow
7m/947 km/h
2 Radon-Ulzer 620C engines

BOLES ROOR
Rust, light yellow
7.39m/790 km/h
2 904E 4-barrel Quadrijets

EBE ENDOCOTT
Light turquoise, light orange
9.55m/785 km/h
2 J930 Dash-8

FINAL BATTLE

LOCATIONS: Plain on Naboo /Palace of Naboo /Theed generator /Space – Vuutun Palaa

LENGTH/BEGINNING : 1.45.06 **END:** 2.04.18 = 19.12 minutes

WHAT'S AT STAKE: stopping the Trade Federation's invasion of Naboo

BEGINNING: Federation fires on the Gungans at 1.46.12

FORCES PRESENT: Gungans vs droid army /Amidala vs Federation /Jedi vs Sith /Naboo fleet vs Federation vessel

KEY CHARACTERS

REPUBLIC

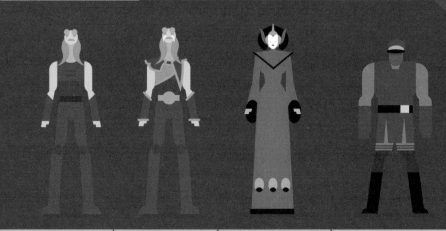

JAR JAR BINKS	ROOS TARPALS	PADMÉ AMIDALA	PANAKA

JEDI · **OTHER** · **SITH** · **FEDERATION**

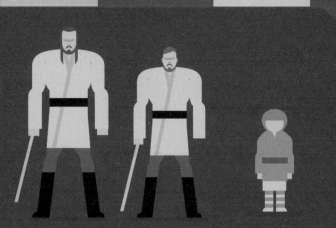

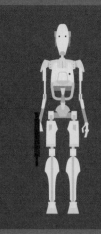

QUI-GON JINN	OBI-WAN KENOBI	ANAKIN SKYWALKER	DARTH MAUL	DROIDS

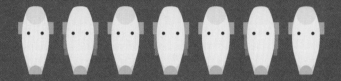

1) CHRONOLOGY AND EVENTS:
PLAIN OF NABOO

Federation's first shot at 1.46.12

Droids deployed at 1.49.16

Droids cross the Gungan shield at 1.49.41

Destruction of the Gungan shield at 1.56.48

Jar Jar and Roos Tarpals are surrounded at 2.00.23

Droids annihilated at 2.03.36

IN BRIEF

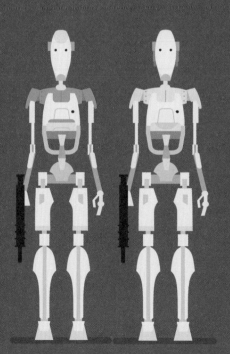

NUMBER OF DROIDS
ON THE GROUND :
10 MTT =
1000+ droids (one MTT =
112 droids or 20 droidekas)

JAR JAR'S GAFFES

falls off mount at 1.49.51

taken out by his own cannonball at 1.50.04

panic attack at 1.53.26

gets his foot stuck in a wire at 1.53.33

picks off 3 droids by accident at 1.53.37

accidentally releases explosive cannonballs at 1.57.17

hides under a vehicle which starts to move at 1.57.03

tries to outrun explosive cannonballs at 1.57.28

lands on the barrel of an AAT at 1.57.45

fails to catch a grenade which destroys a droid at 1.57.56

surrenders like a coward at 2.00.28

2) Chronology and Events:
Palace of Naboo – Theed Hangar

Arrival of Amidala and the Jedi at the Palace of Naboo (in Federation hands) at 1.46.19

First shot against a Federation AAT at 1.46.38

Arrival at the Theed Hangar at 1.47.05

Naboo fighters lift at 1.47.32

 Anakin boards a fighter at 1.47.45

First loss for Naboo: a fighter at 1.47.58

Darth Maul appears at 1.50.26

Amidala's troops split off at 1.50.44

Droidekas arrive at 1.50.48

Anakin powers up his fighter at 1.51.25

Anakin wipes out the droidekas at 1.51.38

Anakin lifts at 1.51.56

Amidala and Panaka go out the window at 1.55.05

Amidala and Panaka arrested at 1.58.26

Queen's decoy appears at 2.00.48
__TURNING POINT__

Amidala retakes control of the palace at 2.01.14

3) Chronology and Events:
Theed Hangar – Theed Generator

Darth Maul ignites his lightsaber at 1.51.02

 Obi-Wan and Qui-Gon ignite theirs at 1.51.05

Interruption of combat at 1.56.21

Qui-Gon is run through at 1.59.55
TURNING POINT

Obi-Wan resumes the fight
at 2.01.30

Obi-Wan breaks Darth Maul's
lightsaber at 2.01.45
Crack!

Obi-Wan falls into the pit and
loses his lightsaber at 02.02.10

Obi-Wan recovers
Qui-Gon's lightsaber at 2.04.17

Cuts Darth Maul in two at 2.04.18

IN BRIEF

Number of lightsaber clashes: 115

4) CHRONOLOGY AND EVENTS:
SPACE – DROID CONTROL CENTRE

Fighter fleet arrives within
range of the Vuutun Palaa: 1.48.07

First shots exchanged at 1.48.20
(Naboo green, Federation red)

Anakin closes on the Vuutun Palaa
at 1.53.10

Anakin lands in the Vuutun
Palaa at 1.59.00

Anakin restarts his fighter at 2.02.25
TURNING POINT

Destruction of a core on Vuutun Palaa
at 2.02.40

Anakin escapes from the Vuutun Palaa at 2.03.20

Vuutun Palaa explodes at 2.03.20

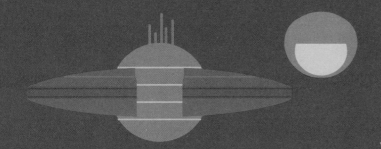

BOOM!

Character Journeys

✕ MYGEETO

✕ ENDOR

OUTER RIM

✕ HOTH

✕ BESPIN

1

1

✕ MUSTAFAR

✕ NABOO

✕ DAGOBAH

✕ UTAPAU

2

2

YAVIN 4  ✕

MID RIM

FELUCIA ✕

EXPANSION
REGION

INNER RIM

COLONIES

1
✕ CORUSCANT

 ✕ ALDERAAN

INNER
CLUSTER

KASHYYYK
✕

1

1

1

3

2

3

4

 ✕ KAMINO

2

2

2

2

3

3

1

✕ TATOOINE

3

1

✕ GEONOSIS

Anakin Skywalker

Padmé Amidala

Obi-Wan Kenobi

C-3PO

R2-D2

Yoda

Palpatine

Jango Fett

FINAL BATTLE

LOCATIONS: Geonosis : Petranaki arena /air and land /Dooku's hangar

LENGTH/BEGINNING : 1.50.03   **END : 2.10.51**   = 20.48 minutes

WHAT'S AT STAKE: destruction of a droid foundry and arrest of Count Dooku

BEGINNING: Windu ignites his lightsaber — **END:** Dooku escapes

FORCES PRESENT: Clone army commanded by Yoda and Jedi council commanded by Windu vs Separatists commanded by Dooku

KEY CHARACTERS

REPUBLIC

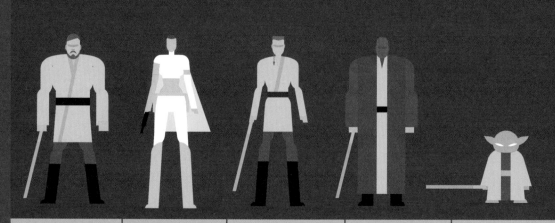

OBI-WAN KENOBI	PADMÉ AMIDALA	ANAKIN SKYWALKER	MACE WINDU	YODA

SEPARATISTS

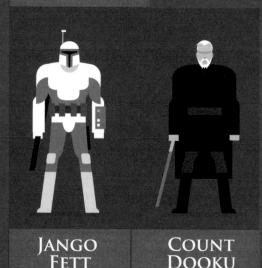

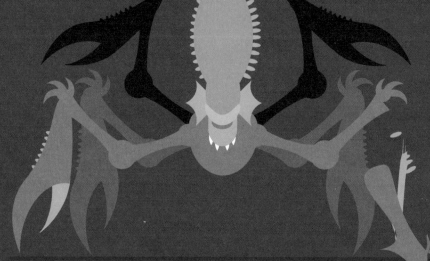

JANGO FETT	COUNT DOOKU

1) Chronology and Events:
Geonosis: Petranaki arena

Mace Windu ignites his lightsaber at 1.50.03

Jedi Council joins the battle at 1.50.14

Separatists open fire at 1.50.42

Jango Fett attacks with a flamethrower at 1.50.45

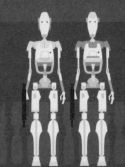

Droid army appears at 1.50.52

Anakin and Obi-Wan recover their lightsabers at 1.51.06

Jango Fett kills a Jedi (Coleman Trebor) at 1.52.28

Mace Windu beheads Jango Fett at 1.53.19

Combat interrupted at 1.55.33

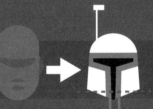

Yoda and the clone army join the battle at 1.56.27
TURNING POINT

In brief

JEDI IN THE ARENA: 20
7 fallen in combat

Number of shots fired by C-3PO: 15

Jango Fett VS Reek

Obi-Wan Kenobi VS Acklay

Reek gores Jango at 1.52.54
Reek tramples Jango at 1.52.58
Jango kills reek at 1.53.08

Obi-Wan kills acklay at 1.54.39
Boba Fett recovers Jango Fett's helmet at 1.57.45

121

2) Chronology and events:
Petranaki arena: air/ground

 **BOOM!** Destruction of a Geonosis reservoir at 1.58.13

 Destruction of a LAAT/i at 1.58.54 **BOOM!**

 Mace Windu takes command on the ground at 1.59.08

Yoda takes command in the air at 1.59.17

Dooku escapes with the plans to the Death Star at 2.01.53

Destruction of a Federation vessel at 2.02.38

 Anakin and Obi-Wan pursue Dooku at 2.03.16

 Amidala falls from the LAAT/i at 2.03.35

 Dooku arrives at his hangar at 2.04.36

 Anakin and Obi-Wan reach the hangar at 2.04.45

 Amidala regains consciousness at 2.06.02

In Brief

  First appearance of the Death Star at 1.58.28 in Dooku's command center

3) CHRONOLOGY AND EVENTS:
DOOKU'S HANGAR

Dooku knocks Anakin down with Force lightning at 2.05.06

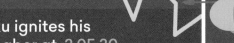

Obi-Wan blocks lightning with his lightsaber at 2.05.20

Dooku ignites his lightsaber at 2.05.30

Anakin regains consciousness at 2.05.55

Dooku wounds Obi-Wan at 2.06.29

Anakin saves Obi-Wan at 2.06.39

Anakin has two lightsabers at 2.06.50

Dooku disarms the green lightsaber at 2.06.57

Dooku cuts off Anakin's arm at 2.07.30

Yoda appears at 2.07.46
TURNING POINT

Yoda reflects Dooku's Force lightning at 2.08.46

Dooku ignites his lightsaber at 2.09.07

Yoda ignites his at 2.09.18

Dooku topples a tank at 2.10.00

Yoda saves Obi-Wan and Anakin at 2.10.15

Amidala reaches the hangar at 2.10.40

Dooku escapes at 2.10.41

IN BRIEF

NUMBER OF CLASHES: 42 (Obi-Wan/Anakin/Dooku) – 28 (Yoda/Dooku)
PROJECTILES DEFLECTED BY YODA: 5
LEAPS PERFORMED BY YODA: 18 in 42 seconds = a leap every 2.33 seconds

MY

OUTER RIM

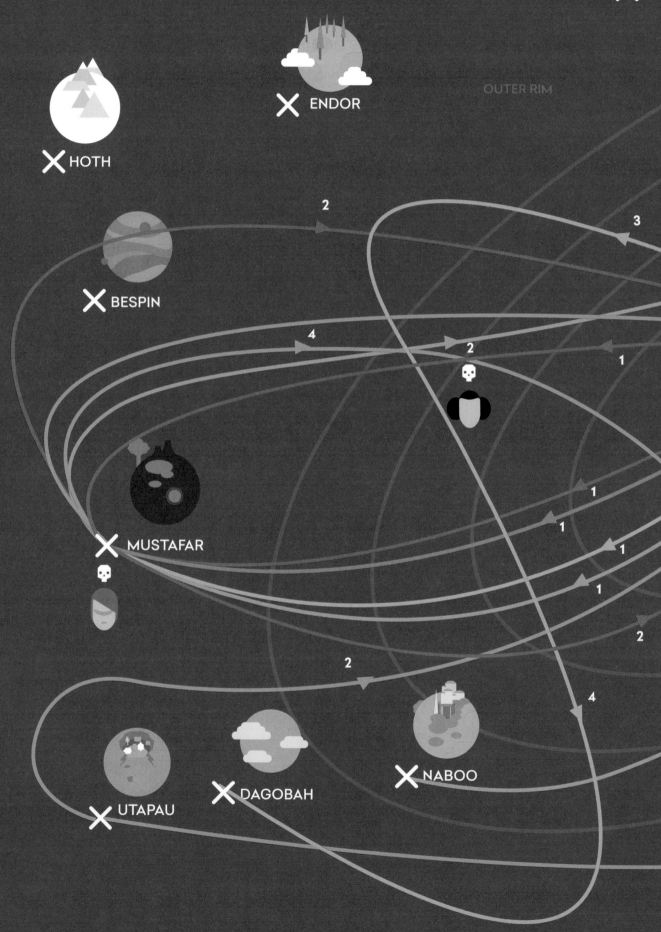

ENDOR

HOTH

BESPIN

2

3

4

2

1

2

1

1

1

1

MUSTAFAR

1

2

2

4

UTAPAU

DAGOBAH

NABOO

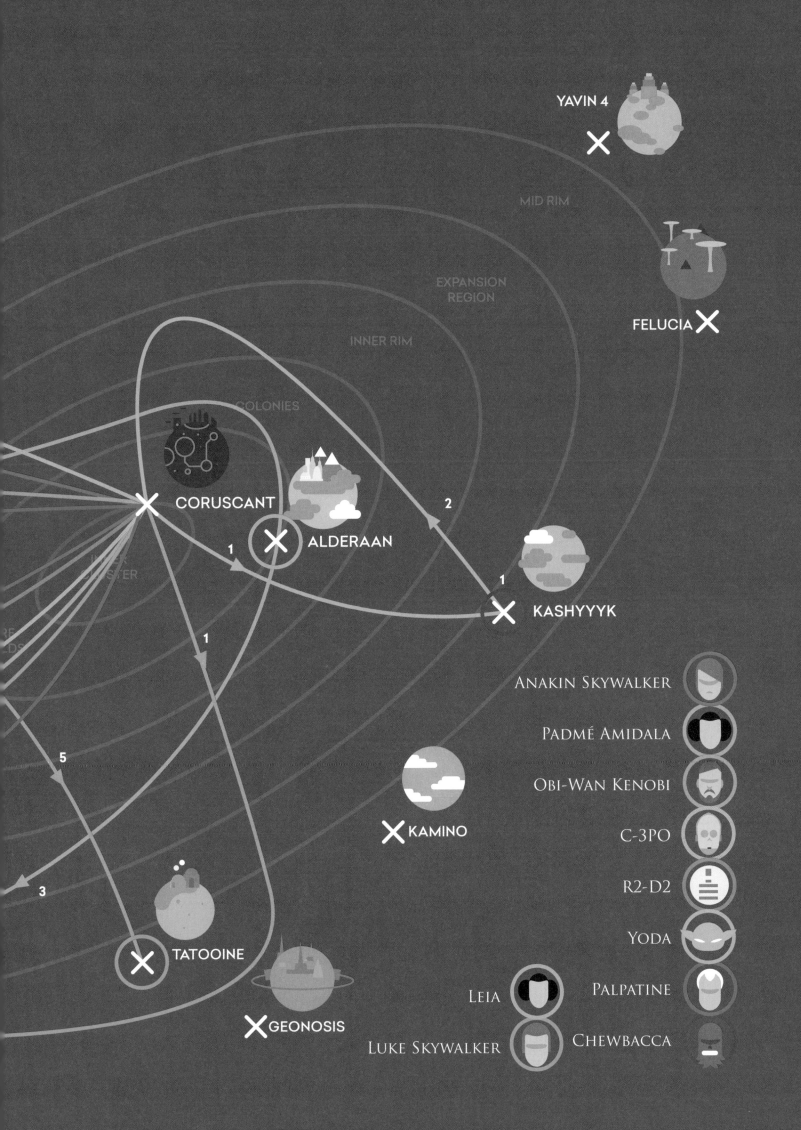

YAVIN 4

MID RIM

EXPANSION
REGION

INNER RIM

FELUCIA

COLONIES

CORUSCANT

ALDERAAN

2

1

KASHYYYK

1

1

Anakin Skywalker

Padmé Amidala

5

Obi-Wan Kenobi

KAMINO

C-3PO

R2-D2

3

Yoda

TATOOINE

Palpatine

Leia

GEONOSIS

Luke Skywalker

Chewbacca

FINAL BATTLE

LOCATION : Mustafar / Coruscant

LENGTH/BEGINNING: 1.46.04 **END: 1.59.37** **= 13.33 minutes**

BEGINNING: appearance of Obi-Wan

END: Anakin's legs cut off/Yoda falls

FORCES PRESENT: Jedi VS Sith

KEY CHARACTERS

REPUBLIC

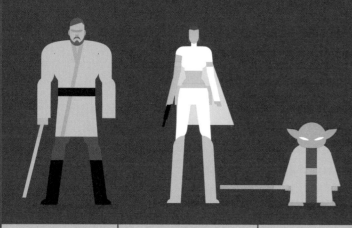

SITH

IN TRANSITION

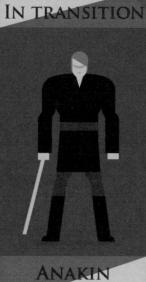

| OBI-WAN KENOBI | PADMÉ AMIDALA | YODA | DARTH SIDIOUS | ANAKIN SKYWALKER |

1) CHRONOLOGY AND EVENTS:
MUSTAFAR

Obi-Wan appears at 1.46.04

Anakin Force-chokes Amidala at 1.46.17

Anakin drops his cloak at 1.46.46

Obi-Wan drops his cloak at 1.46.51

Obi-Wan ignites first at 1.47.53

Anakin ignites at 1.47.54

First clash at 1.47.56

they go indoors

Anakin strangles
Obi-Wan at 1.50.57

Force vs Force at 1.52.04

Steam pipes at 1.52.18

outdoors

Obi-Wan lands on the
river of lava at 1.57.37

Anakin lands on the river
of lava at 1.57.55

Obi-Wan leaps from his platform, returns to solid
ground and gains the upper hand at 1.59.16
TURNING POINT

Anakin leaps off his
platform at 1.59.35

Obi-Wan cuts off Anakin's arm
and legs at 1.59.37

IN BRIEF

LIGHTSABER CLASHES:
168

KICKS :
7

2) CHRONOLOGY AND EVENTS:
UNDER THE SENATE/IN THE SENATE

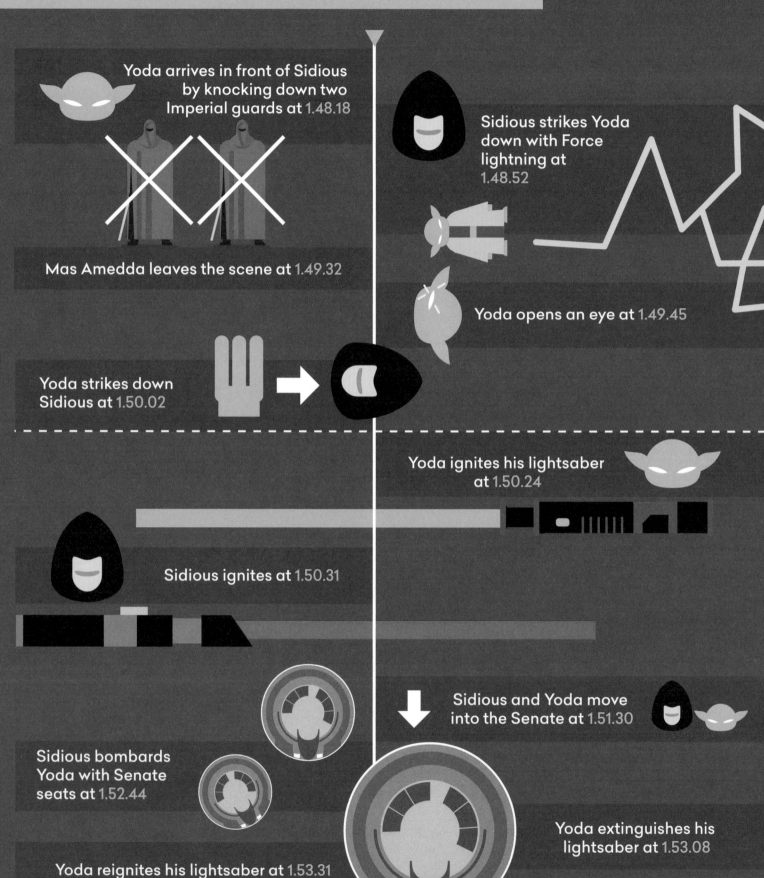

Yoda arrives in front of Sidious by knocking down two Imperial guards at 1.48.18

Sidious strikes Yoda down with Force lightning at 1.48.52

Mas Amedda leaves the scene at 1.49.32

Yoda opens an eye at 1.49.45

Yoda strikes down Sidious at 1.50.02

Yoda ignites his lightsaber at 1.50.24

Sidious ignites at 1.50.31

Sidious and Yoda move into the Senate at 1.51.30

Sidious bombards Yoda with Senate seats at 1.52.44

Yoda extinguishes his lightsaber at 1.53.08

Yoda reignites his lightsaber at 1.53.31

Sidious disarms Yoda with Force lightning at 1.53.36
TURNING POINT

Lightning duel at 1.53.36

BOOM!

Force explosion at 1.53.52

BOOM!

BOOM!

Yoda falls at 1.54.05

IN BRIEF

LIGHTSABER CLASHES : 40

DARTH SIDIOUS
LEAPS PERFORMED : 2

YODA
LEAPS PERFORMED : 24
PROJECTILES AVOIDED: 6
PROJECTILE RETURNED: 1

CHARACTER COSTUMES THROUGH THE FILMS

Obi-Wan Kenobi [total : 1]

Ep. I : 1
Ep. II : 1
Ep. III : 1

Qui-Gon Jinn [total : 1]

Ep. I : 1

Anakin Skywalker [total : 6]

Ep. I : 3
Ep. II : 2
Ep. III : 1

Padmé Amidala [total : 36]

Ep. I : 10
Ep. II : 15
Ep. III : 11

Jar-Jar Binks [total : 3]

Ep. I : 1
Ep. II : 1
Ep. III : 1

Palpatine [total : 12]

Ep. I : 2
Ep. II : 3
Ep. III : 7

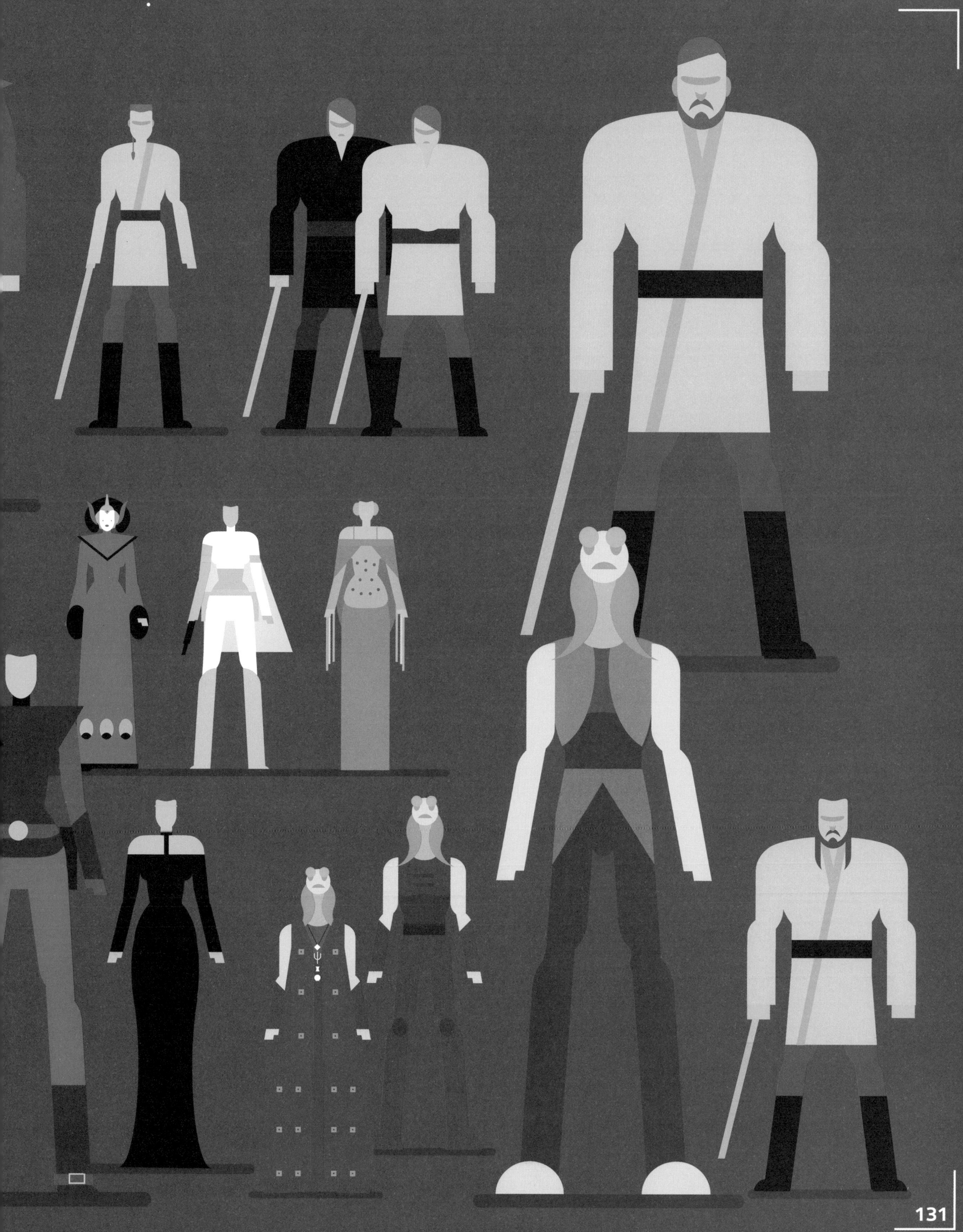

STAR WARS™

THE FORCE AWAKENS
GRAPHICS

THE FORCE AWAKENS
IN NUMBERS

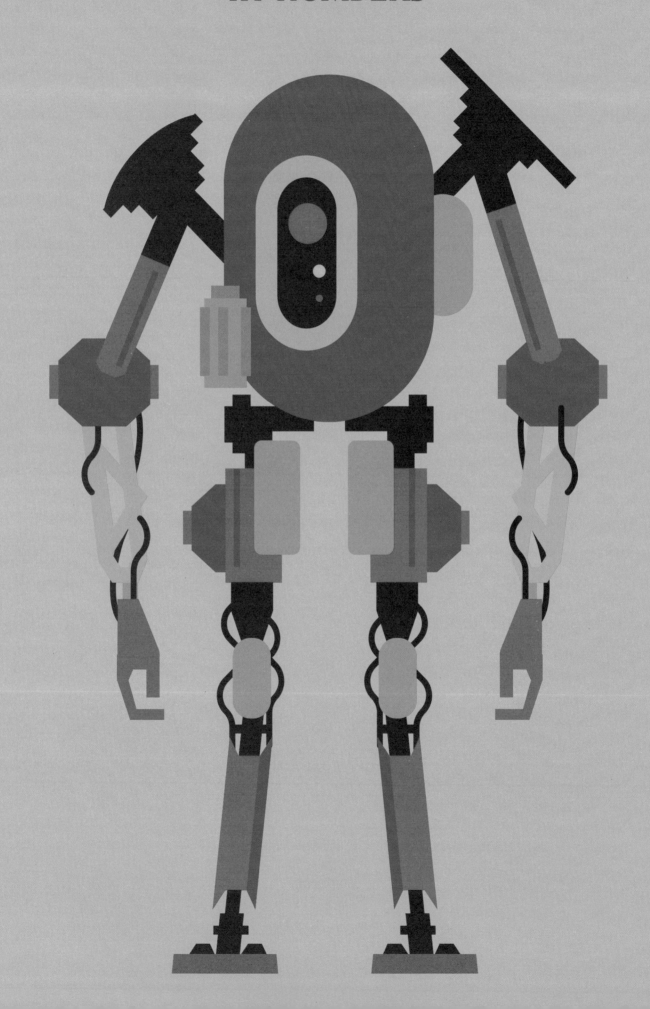

3 HEROES

1 LIGHTSABER

1 SPEEDER

2 BASES

1 SON

1 JEDI

3 LIGHTSABER BATTLES

2 GENERALS

1 LEADER OF THE FIRST ORDER

2 MERCENARY GANGS

1 DESERTER

1 MILLENNIUM FALCON

1 MAZ KANATA

3 RATHTARS

CHARACTER JOURNEYS

The heroes of the *Star Wars* Universe have always hopped from planet to planet. Here's a brief look at the characters in action in *The Force Awakens*.

TAKODANA

FIRST ORDER SHIP

ERAVANA

JAKKU

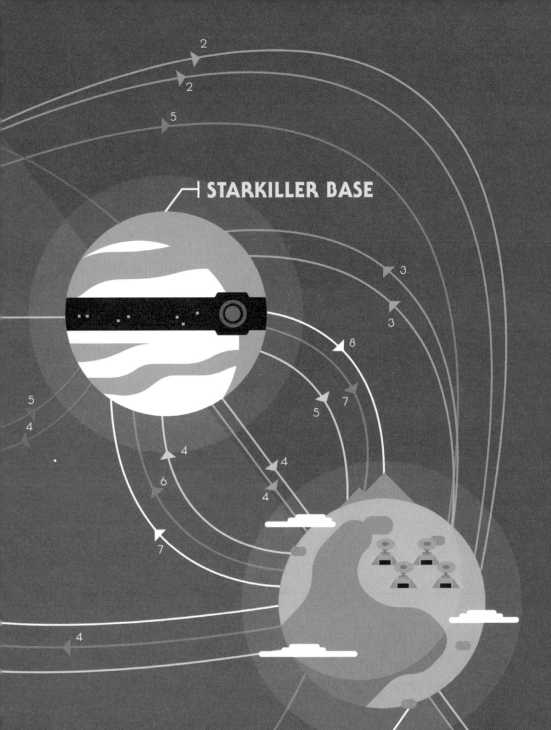

STARKILLER BASE

2

2

5

3

3

8

5

7

5

4

5

4

6

4

4

7

4

D'QAR

5

5

AHCH-TO

HAN SOLO

CHEWBACCA

KYLO REN

REY

FINN

BB-8

POE DAMERON

THE EVOLUTION OF
C-3PO

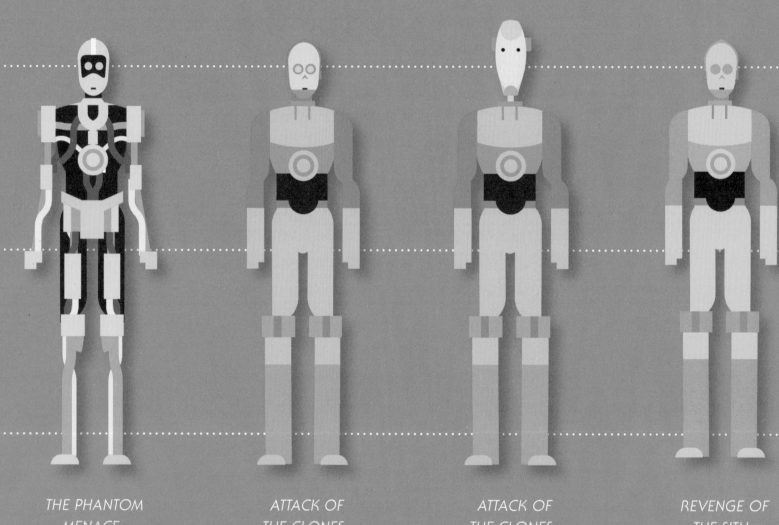

THE PHANTOM
MENACE

ATTACK OF
THE CLONES

ATTACK OF
THE CLONES

REVENGE OF
THE SITH

C-3PO is a legendary figure in the saga, largely due to his unique and instantly recognisable physical appearance. And yet, the famously rule-abiding droid has changed numerous times. The details of some of these transformations can be seen below.

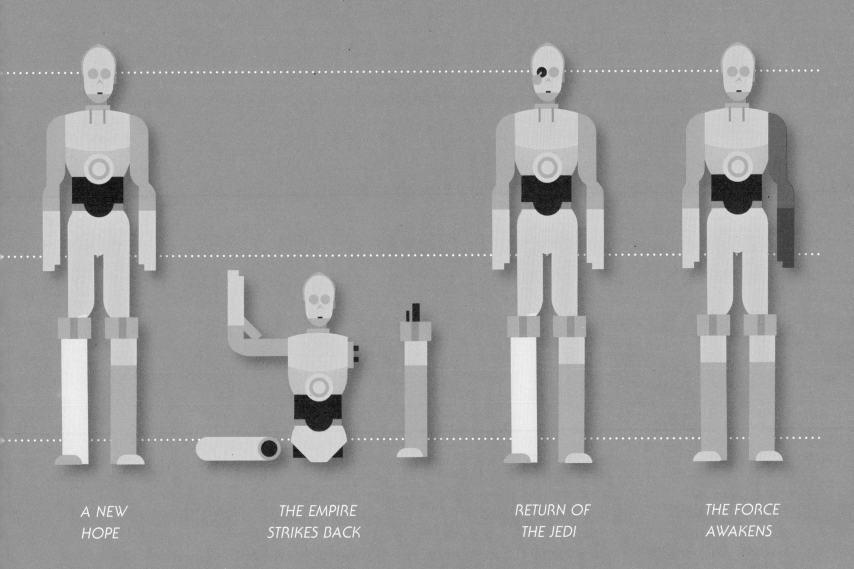

A NEW
HOPE

THE EMPIRE
STRIKES BACK

RETURN OF
THE JEDI

THE FORCE
AWAKENS

DROID
GENERATIONS

BB-8

TYPE	ASTROMECH
CATEGORY	BB SERIES
MANNED SPACECRAFT	X-WING T-70
EQUIPMENT	ATTACHMENT CABLES
	WELDING TORCH
	HOLOPROJECTOR
	ARC WELDER
	-
	-
	DATA COLLECTOR
	ALL TERRAIN
MASTERS	POE DAMERON

Like R2-D2, BB-8 is a trusty and charming droid who, with a few beeps and whistles, steals the show. Here is a look at how the two droids compare.

R2-D2

- ASTROMECH
- R2 SERIES
- DELTA-7B - ETA 2 INTERCEPTOR - X-WING T-65 - Y-WING
- -
- WELDING TORCH
- HOLOPROJECTOR
- ARC WELDER
- LIGHTSABER COMPARTMENT
- PERISCOPE
- DATA COLLECTOR
- ALL TERRAIN
- PADMÉ AMIDALA - ANAKIN SKYWALKER - BAIL ORGANA - OWEN LARS - LUKE SKYWALKER

FAMILY TREE
FROM SHMI TO KYLO REN

Adoption

Love

Bloodline

Beru Whitesun

Cliegg Lars

Owen Lars

Luke Skywalker

Shmi Skywalker

Anakin Skywalker

Breha Organa

Padmé Amidala

Leia Organa

Kylo Ren

Bail Organa

Han Solo

THE LIGHTSABER'S JOURNEY
THE STORY OF A ROUND TRIP

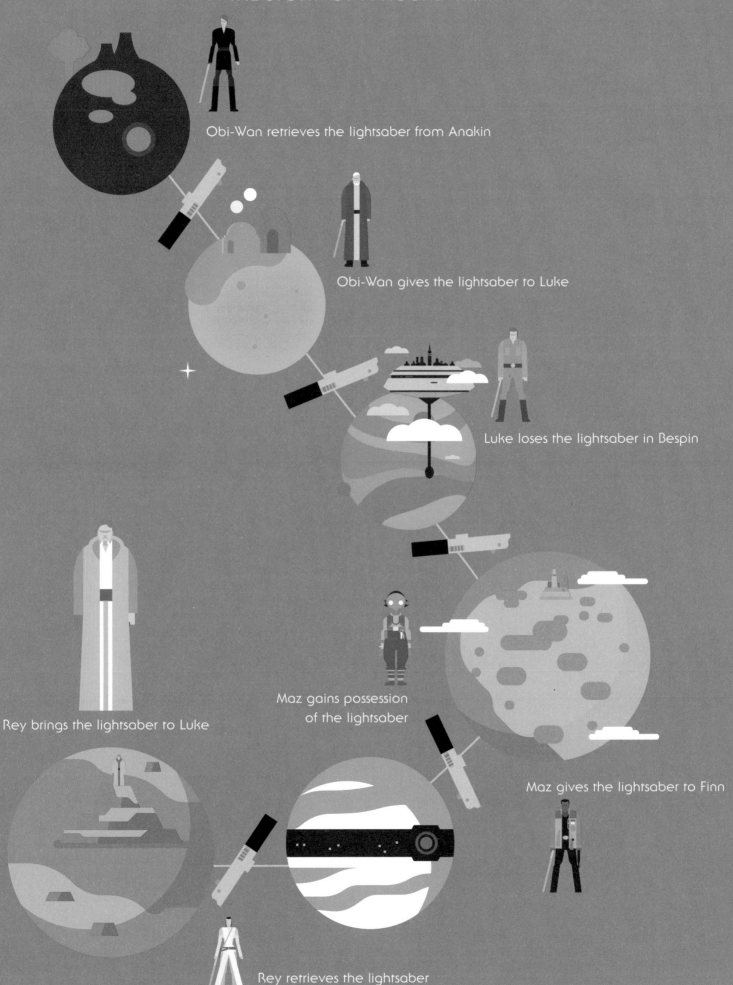

Obi-Wan retrieves the lightsaber from Anakin

Obi-Wan gives the lightsaber to Luke

Luke loses the lightsaber in Bespin

Rey brings the lightsaber to Luke

Maz gains possession of the lightsaber

Maz gives the lightsaber to Finn

Rey retrieves the lightsaber

PHYSICAL PROPORTIONS
FROM THE DEATH STAR TO STARKILLER

The Empire's army evolved into the First Order, which inherited its predecessor's ability to construct gigantic battle stations. How does the base built by Palpatine's army compare to that of the ghostly Snoke?

DEATH STAR

DEATH STAR II

STARKILLER BASE

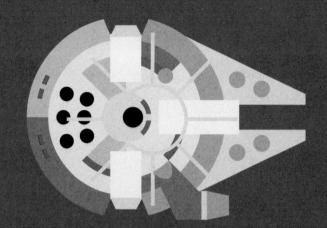

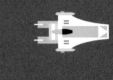

EPISODE I
THE PHANTOM MENACE
32 BBY

EPISODE III
REVENGE OF THE SITH
19 BBY

EPISODE V
THE EMPIRE STRIKES BACK
3 ABY

EPISODE II
ATTACK OF THE CLONES
22 BBY

EPISODE IV
A NEW HOPE
0 ABY

EPISODE VI
RETURN OF THE JEDI
4 ABY

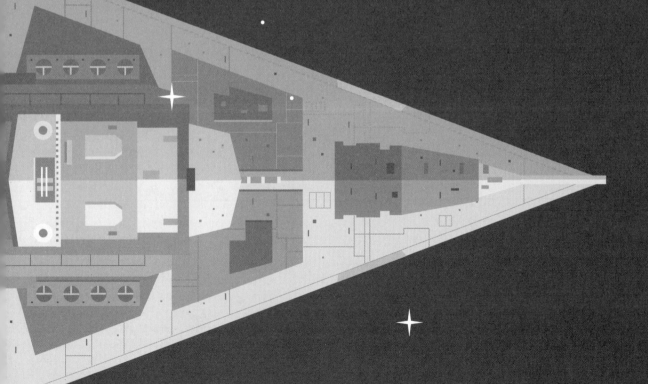

THE STAR WARS TIMELINE

Our heroes have grown and changed, but how long has it been?
And how much time has passed since the Battle of Yavin in *A New Hope*?

BBY = Before the Battle of Yavin   ABY = After the Battle of Yavin

EPISODE VII
THE FORCE AWAKENS
34 ABY

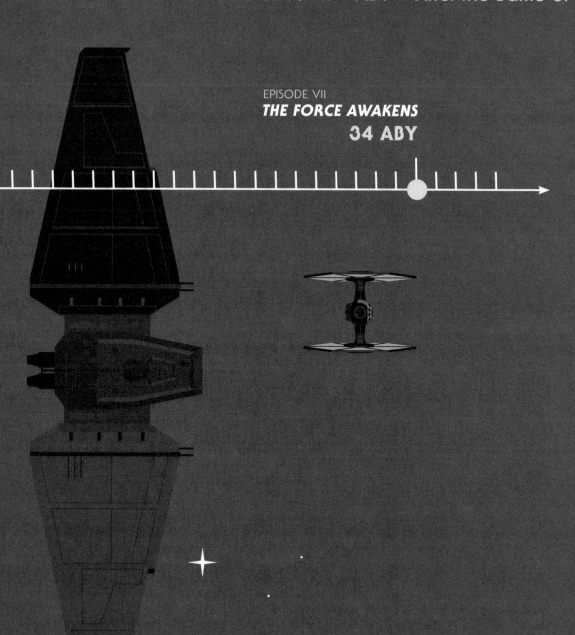

KYLO REN

Kylo Ren fancies himself as the successor to his illustrious forebear, but does he possess the same qualities as Darth Vader?

FATHER — HAN SOLO

MOTHER — LEIA ORGANA

MASTER (LIGHT SIDE OF THE FORCE) — LUKE SKYWALKER

MASTER (DARK SIDE OF THE FORCE) — SNOKE

AFFILIATION — KNIGHTS OF REN

NUMBER OF DUELS SHOWN

Finn   Rey

ARTIFICIAL LIMBS
0

NUMBER OF LIGHTSABER BLADES

III

FILMS

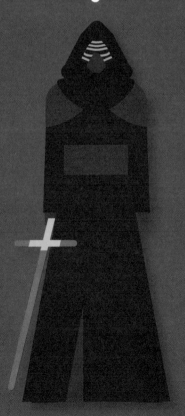

DARTH VADER

FATHER — NONE

MOTHER — SHMI SKYWALKER

MASTER (LIGHT SIDE OF THE FORCE) — OBI-WAN KENOBI

MASTER (DARK SIDE OF THE FORCE) — PALPATINE

AFFILIATION — SITH

NUMBER OF DUELS SHOWN

X X X
Obi-Wan   Luke   Luke

NUMBER OF LIGHTSABER BLADES

FILMS

ARTIFICIAL LIMBS
4

CHARACTER QUOTES

Han Solo

Chewie ... we're home.

Chewbacca

We'll figure it out. We'll use the Force.

Finn

You're Han Solo?

Stop taking my hand!

Rey

In the world of *Star Wars*, things quickly gain cult status, even what the characters say. In *The Force Awakens*, there are the usual references to missing droids and the recurring 'I have a bad feeling about this', but some new quotes have joined the fray. Here are a select few.

Kylo Ren

Snoke

There has been an awakening ... have you felt it?

I will finish what you started.

You need a pilot!

Poe Dameron

Darth Vader's helmet

Rey, may the Force be with you.

Excuse me, Princess ... General ... Sorry!

Leia

C-3PO

KYLO REN'S
RAGES

Kylo Ren is a sombre and mysterious character with an infamous lineage; however, he is incapable of controlling his anger. Here we return to the notable moments where Kylo Ren lost control.

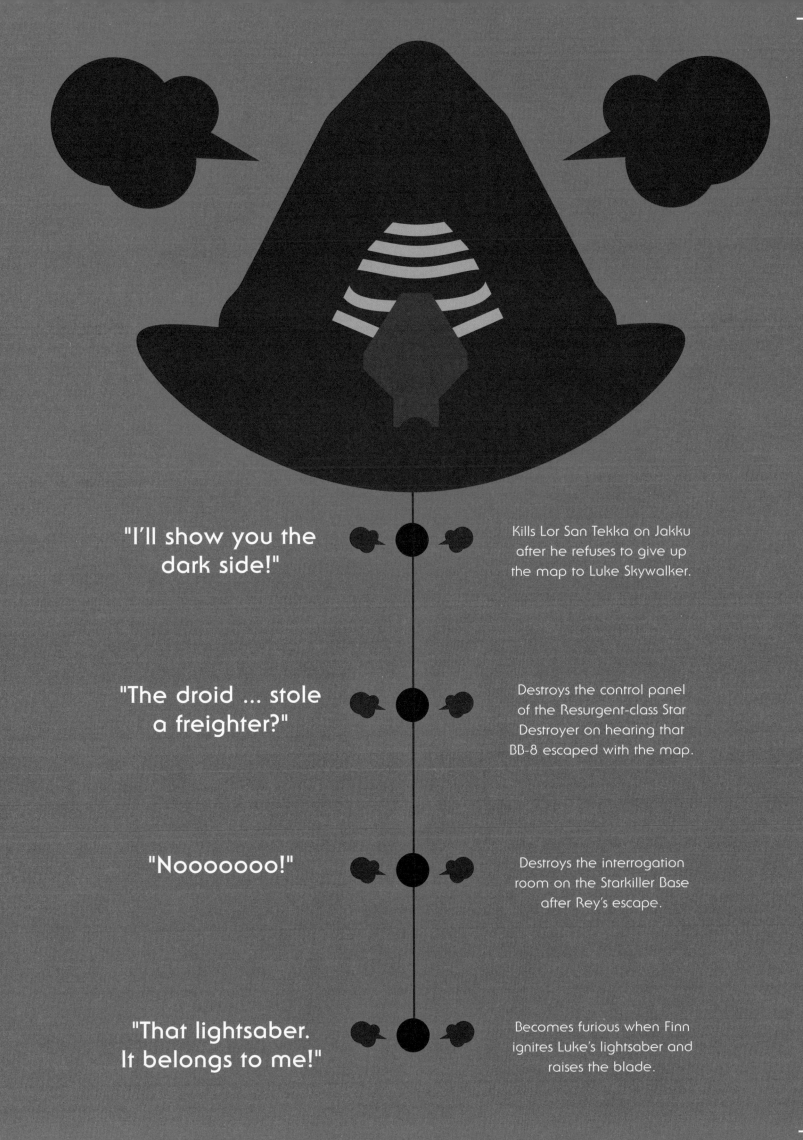

"I'll show you the dark side!"

Kills Lor San Tekka on Jakku after he refuses to give up the map to Luke Skywalker.

"The droid ... stole a freighter?"

Destroys the control panel of the Resurgent-class Star Destroyer on hearing that BB-8 escaped with the map.

"Nooooooo!"

Destroys the interrogation room on the Starkiller Base after Rey's escape.

"That lightsaber. It belongs to me!"

Becomes furious when Finn ignites Luke's lightsaber and raises the blade.

CHARACTER
MEASUREMENTS

Happabore
2.30 M

Han Solo
1.80 M

Poe Dameron
1.74 M

Luke Skywalker
1.72 M

Rey
1.70 M

Maz Kanata
1.24 M

Chewbacca
2.28 M

Finn
1.78 M

Leia Organa
1.50 M

C-3PO
1.71 M

R2-D2
1.09 M

BB-8
67 CM

Snoke
?

Unkar Plutt
1.80 M

Kylo Ren
1.89 M

General Hux
1.85 M

Captain Phasma
2.00 M

CHARACTER
MEASUREMENTS

Grummgar
2.70 M

Stormtrooper
1.83 M

Bala-Tik
1.80 M

Tasu Leech
1.57 M

Bazine Netal
1.70 M

CHARACTER TIES

From the original trilogy to *The Force Awakens*,
history mirrors itself ... but not completely.

LUKE SKYWALKER - - - - - - - - - → REY

HAN SOLO - - - - - → POE DAMERON

R2-D2 - - - - - - - - - → BB-8

OBI-WAN - - - - - - - - - → HAN SOLO

MAZ KANATA - - - - - → YODA

DARTH VADER - - - - - - - → KYLO REN

THE EMPEROR - - - - - - - → SNOKE

GRAND
MOFF TARKIN - - - - - - - → GENERAL HUX

SARLACC - - - - - - → RATHTAR

DEATH STAR - - - - - → STARKILLER BASE

FILMING
LOCATIONS

KRAFLA
ICELAND

STARKILLER

TAKODONA

CUMBRIA
UNITED KINGDOM

AHCH-TO

D'QAR

SKELLIG MICHAEL
IRELAND

GREENHAM COMMON
UNITED KINGDOM

Did you recognise any of the shooting locations while watching *The Force Awakens*? Here is a handy map of the locations that form the backdrop of the new film.

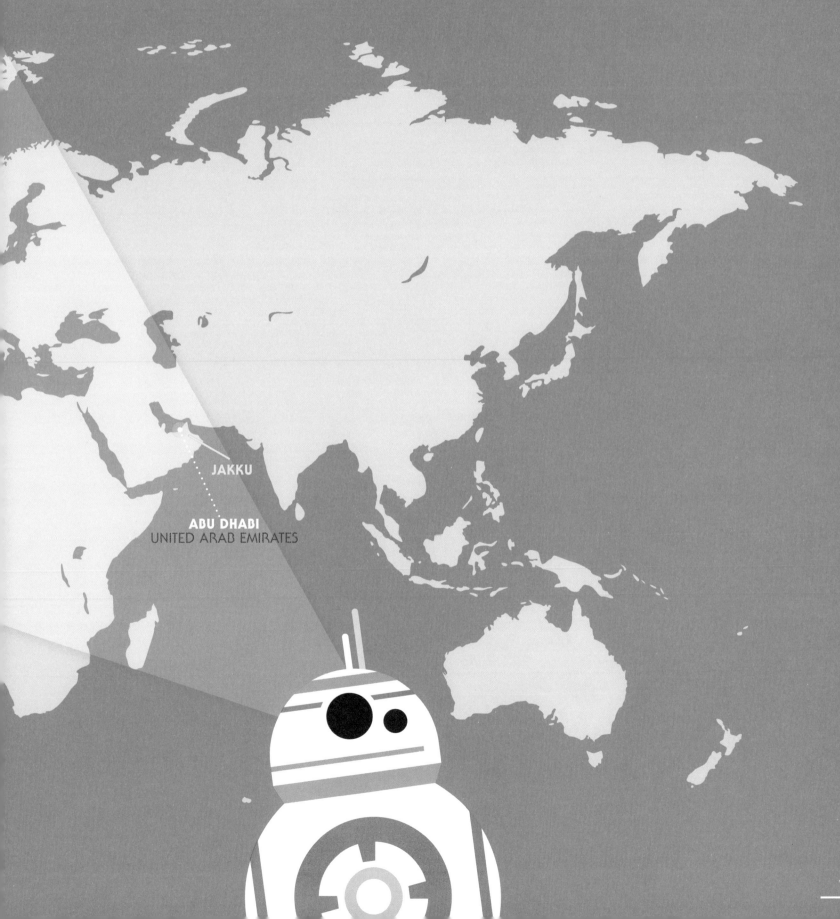

JAKKU

ABU DHABI
UNITED ARAB EMIRATES

NEW PLANETS

The Force Awakens introduced us to new worlds in the Star Wars universe, from a remote desert planet to a mobile ice planet.

JAKKU
LOCATION: INNER RIM
LANDMARK: NIIMA OUTPOST

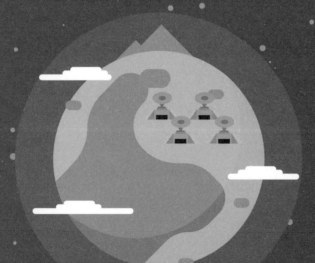

D'QAR
LOCATION: OUTER RIM
LANDMARK: RESISTANCE OUTPOST

TAKODANA
LOCATION: MID RIM
LANDMARK: MAZ KANATA'S CASTLE

HOSNIAN PRIME
LOCATION: CORE WORLD
LANDMARK: CAPITAL OF THE NEW REPUBLIC

AHCH-TO
LOCATION: ?
LANDMARK: ANCIENT RUINS

STARKILLER BASE
LOCATION: UNKNOWN REGIONS
LANDMARK: FIRST ORDER BASE

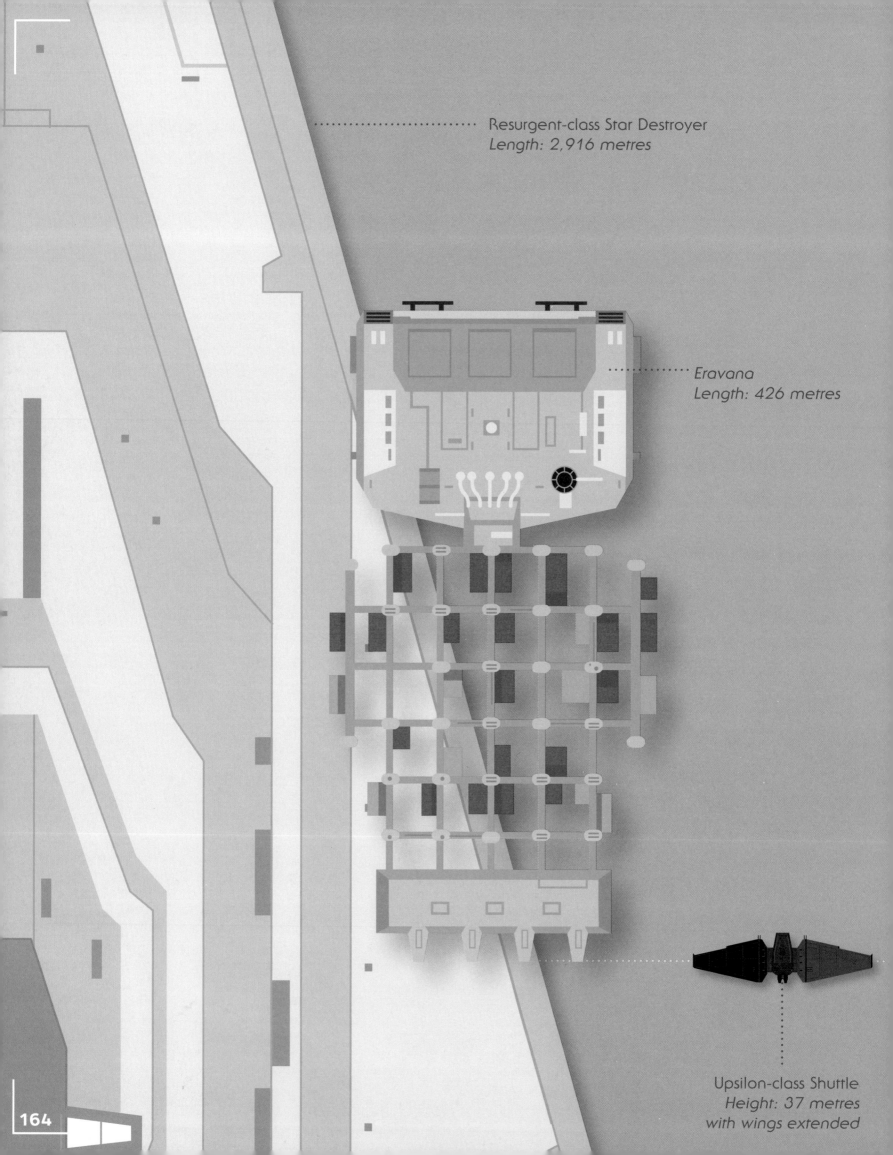

Resurgent-class Star Destroyer
Length: 2,916 metres

Eravana
Length: 426 metres

Upsilon-class Shuttle
*Height: 37 metres
with wings extended*

SPACECRAFT PROPORTIONS

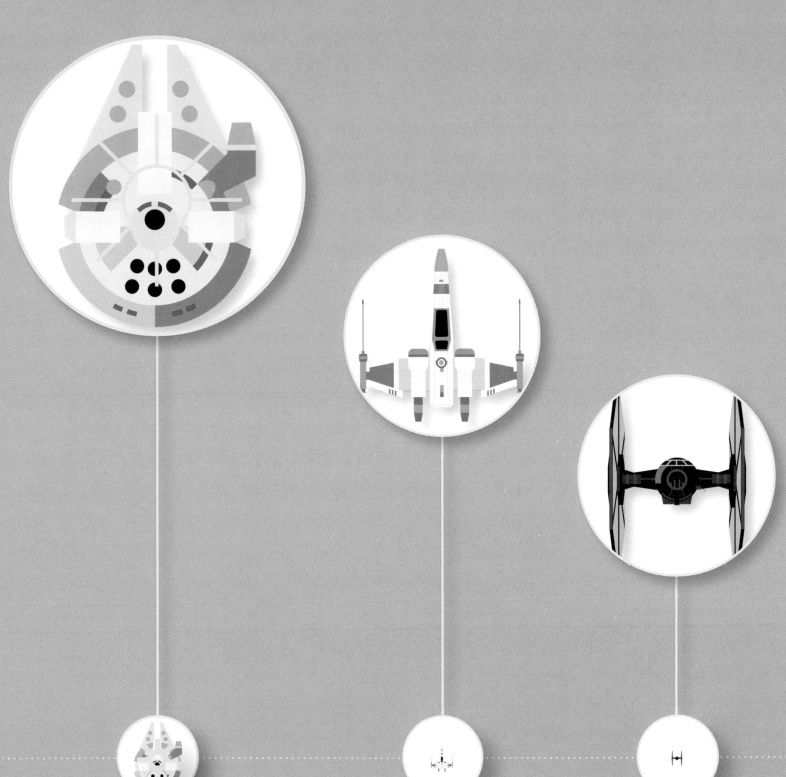

Millennium Falcon
Length: 35 metres

X-wing T-70
Length: 12.5 metres

TIE fighter
Length: 6.7 metres

HUMANOIDS
AND OTHERS

This distant galaxy is teeming with numerous species. Based on the new characters introduced, here is a look at how the species are divided, calculated using the number of characters who have direct interaction with the heroes.

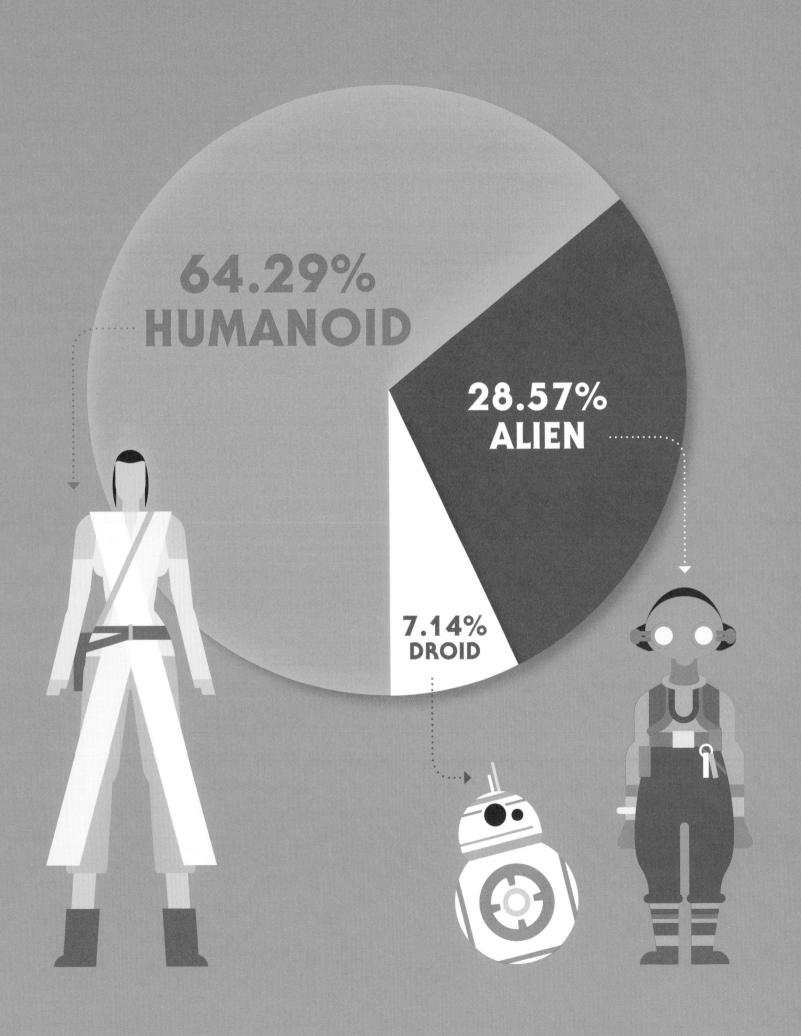

64.29%
HUMANOID

28.57%
ALIEN

7.14%
DROID

1

PHASE 1 CLONE TROOPER
REPUBLIC

EVOLUTION OF
STORMTROOPER
HELMETS

2

PHASE 2 CLONE TROOPER
REPUBLIC

3

STORMTROOPER
EMPIRE

PILOT   SCOUT TROOPER   SNOWTROOPER

FLAMETROOPER

PILOT   SNOWTROOPER

STORMTROOPER
FIRST ORDER

X-WING VS X-WING

X-WING T-65

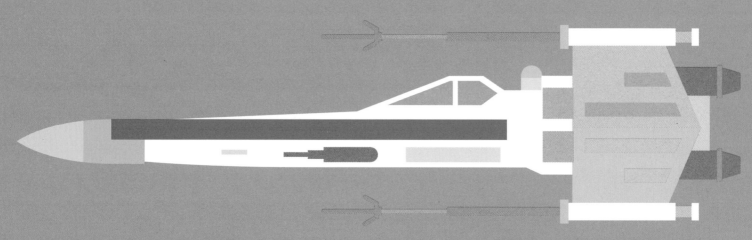

12.50 M LENGTH

 ENGINES

☒ HYPERDRIVE

☒ DEFLECTOR SHIELDS

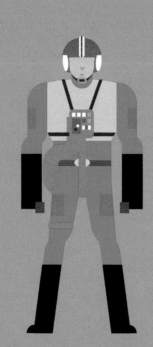

WEDGE ANTILLES

The X-wing fighters – and their stalwart pilots – were crucial to the Rebel Alliance in the Battle of Yavin and the Battle of Endor. In *The Force Awakens*, the Resistance's new X-wing fighter makes its debut.

X-WING T-70

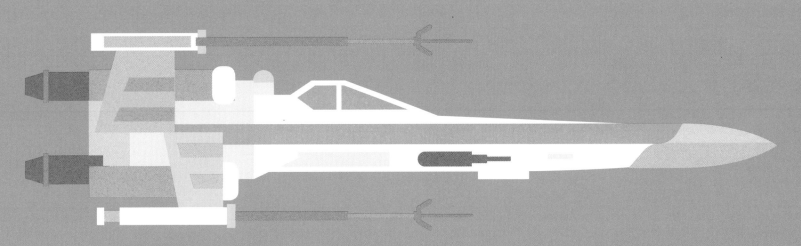

LENGTH 12.48 M

ENGINES ●●●●

HYPERDRIVE ☒

DEFLECTOR SHIELDS ☒

SNAP WEXLEY

TIE FIGHTER VS TIE FIGHTER

Has the exceptional combat craft significantly evolved since the fall of the Empire?

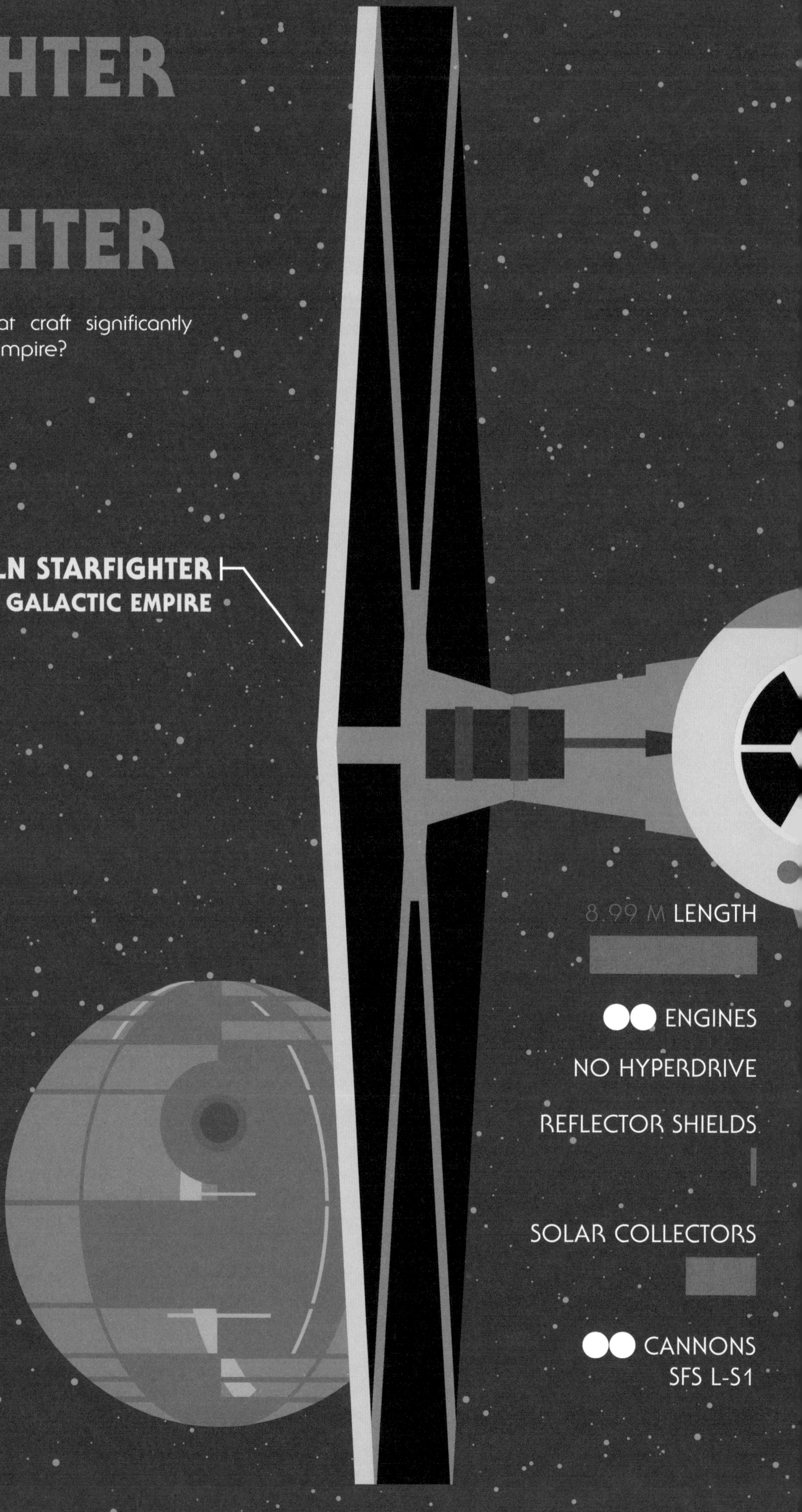

TIE/LN STARFIGHTER
AFFILIATION: GALACTIC EMPIRE

8.99 M LENGTH

●● ENGINES

NO HYPERDRIVE

REFLECTOR SHIELDS

SOLAR COLLECTORS

●● CANNONS
SFS L-S1

LENGTH 6.69 M

ENGINES

NO HYPERDRIVE

REFLECTOR SHIELDS

SOLAR COLLECTORS

CANNONS ●●
S-JFS S9.6

TIE/SF STARFIGHTER
AFFILIATION: FIRST ORDER

THE FINAL BATTLE

What finally led to the downfall of the terrifying First Order army?

1 - Han Solo, Chewbacca and Finn block the Starkiller Base's shields.

2 - Rey escapes from prison and comes across Han Solo, Chewbacca and Finn.

3 - Kylo Ren kills Han Solo. Chewbacca detonates the mines he laid.

4 - Poe Dameron and BB-8 attack the Starkiller Base.

5 - Finn and Rey fight Kylo Ren.
6 - Chewbacca rescues Finn and Rey just before
    the explosion of the Starkiller Base.

UNKAR PLUTT'S
FINANCES

Surviving in the arid deserts of Jakku isn't easy; selling bits and pieces found among the wreckages littering the planet is the best way to make a living. Unkar Plutt takes these scraps in exchange for ration packs. Let's take a closer look at the prices demanded by the horrid Crolute.

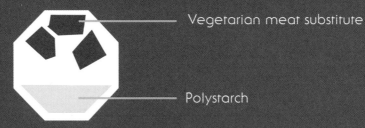

Vegetarian meat substitute

Polystarch

SURVIVAL RATIONS
Stocks from the Republic
and the Empire

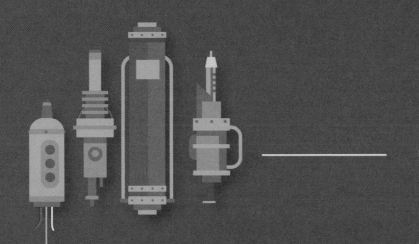

ONE QUARTER RATION

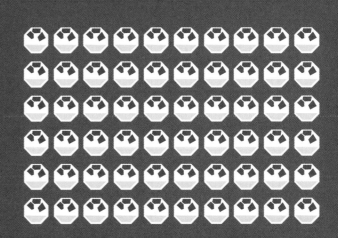

SIXTY RATIONS

CHARACTER OUTFITS
IN *THE FORCE AWAKENS*

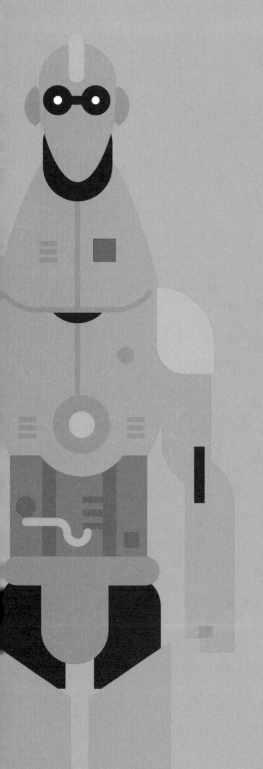

FINN — Stormtrooper uniform • Poe's Jacket

REY — Desert robes

KYLO REN — Armour

HAN SOLO — Leather jacket • Winter coat

POE DAMERON — Jacket • X-wing pilot's uniform

CAPTAIN PHASMA — Armour

LEIA ORGANA — Military uniform • Dress

GENERAL HUX — Military uniform

SUPREME LEADER
SNOKE

KYLO REN

GENERAL HUX

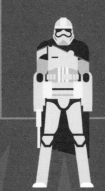

CAPTAIN PHASMA

STORMTROOPERS

THE
HIERARCHY
OF THE FIRST ORDER

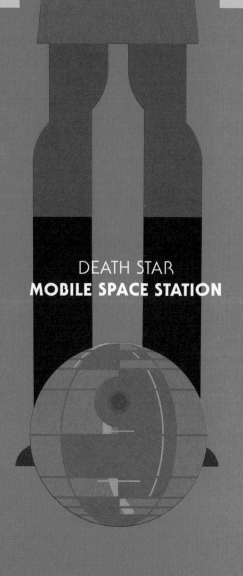

Despite his youth, General Hux rules the Starkiller Base and its garrison with an iron fist. But how does he compare to his infamous predecessor?

GRAND MOFF TARKIN

PALPATINE	**SUPERIOR**
EMPIRE	**ARMY**
GRAND MOFF	**GRADE**
DEATH STAR	**BASE**

DEATH STAR
MOBILE SPACE STATION

RESPONSIBLE FOR THE DESTRUCTION OF:

Alderaan

LOSES TRYING TO DESTROY:

Yavin 4

AFTER HIS DEFEAT:

Dead

GENERAL HUX

SUPERIOR — SNOKE

ARMY — FIRST ORDER

GRADE — GENERAL

BASE — STARKILLER BASE

RESPONSIBLE FOR THE DESTRUCTION OF:

The Hosnian
system

LOSES TRYING TO DESTROY:

D'Qar

AFTER HIS DEFEAT:

Alive

STARKILLER BASE
ICE PLANET

REY
GETS BY ALONE

The young Rey doesn't need anyone's help.
Here we look back at her journey.

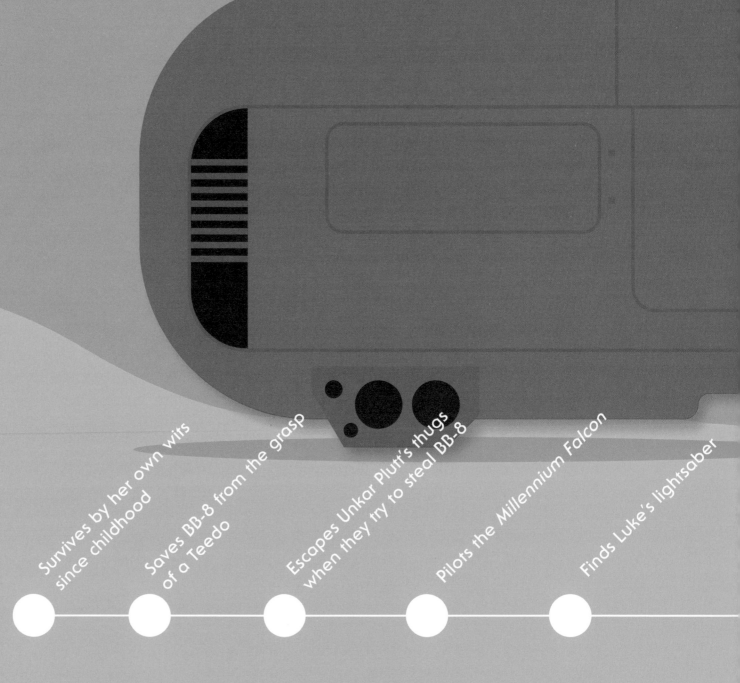

Survives by her own wits since childhood

Saves BB-8 from the grasp of a Teedo

Escapes Unkar Plutt's thugs when they try to steal BB-8

Pilots the Millennium Falcon

Finds Luke's lightsaber

Masters the Force

Escapes from prison

Fights Kylo Ren

Finds Luke Skywalker

EPISODE VIII

TRAILERS & TEASERS

The release of the first trailer announcing the new *Star Wars* film caused a stir, but just how much hype was there?

THE FIRST TEASER TOTALLED

55,000,000

VIEWS IN

24 HOURS

THE SECOND TEASER TOTALLED

88,000,000

VIEWS IN

24 HOURS

THE FIRST TRAILER TOTALLED

128,000,000

VIEWS IN

24 HOURS

=

2 TIMES THE POPULATION OF THE UNITED KINGDOM

15 TIMES THE POPULATION OF NEW YORK

THE STORY OF
HAN SOLO
& LEIA

One fiery meeting gave birth to a magnificent
love story. Here is the touching journey of the
legendary couple.

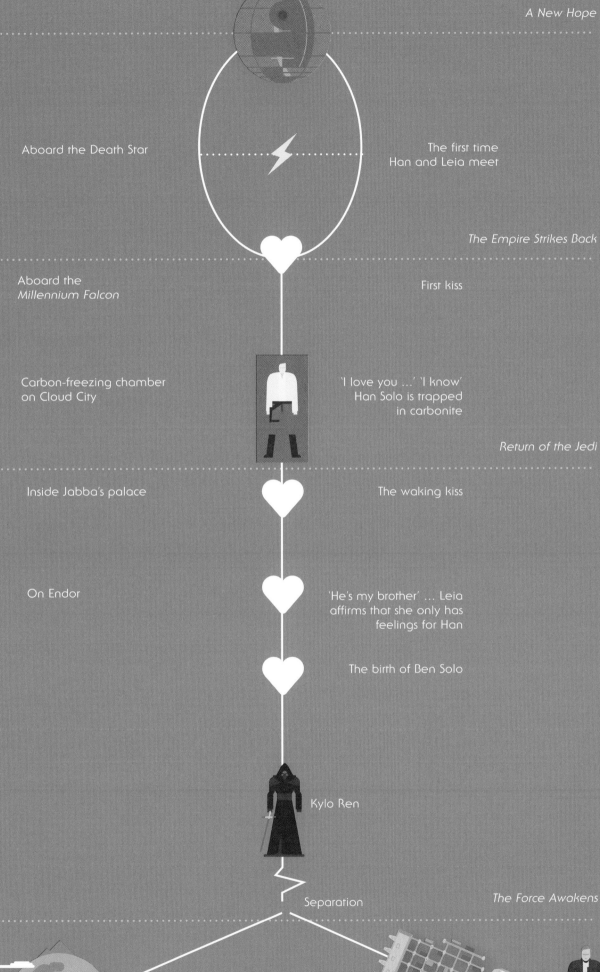

A New Hope

Aboard the Death Star

The first time
Han and Leia meet

The Empire Strikes Back

Aboard the
Millennium Falcon

First kiss

Carbon-freezing chamber
on Cloud City

'I love you ...' 'I know'
Han Solo is trapped
in carbonite

Return of the Jedi

Inside Jabba's palace

The waking kiss

On Endor

'He's my brother' ... Leia
affirms that she only has
feelings for Han

The birth of Ben Solo

Kylo Ren

Separation

The Force Awakens

Takodana

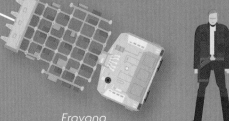

Eravana

THE ASTROMECH FAMILY

FROM R-SERIES TO BB

R-SERIES

Versatile astromech droid line, particularly popular with pilots.

R-SERIES

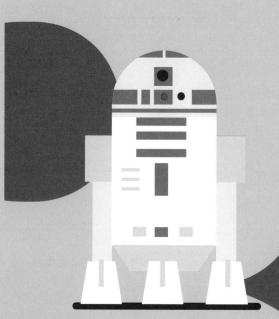

R-SERIES

R-SERIES

R-SERIES

R-SERIES

R-SERIES

C-SERIES

Protocol droids programmed with many forms of communication.

C-SERIES

Before BB-8, there was a line of R-series astromechs – R2-D2 is the most famous example – as well as the C-Series. This page shows the progression of astromech droids to which BB-8 owes everything.

R-SERIES

BB-SERIES